CULTURE SMART!

ETHIOPIA

Sarah Howard

·K·U·P·E·R·A·R·D·

ISBN 978 1 85733 494 4
This book is also available as an e-book: eISBN 978 1 85733 603 0

British Library Cataloguing in Publication Data
A CIP catalogue entry for this book is available from the British Library

First published in Great Britain
by Kuperard, an imprint of Bravo Ltd
59 Hutton Grove, London N12 8DS
Tel: +44 (0) 20 8446 2440   Fax: +44 (0) 20 8446 2441
www.culturesmart.co.uk
Inquiries: sales@kuperard.co.uk

Distributed in the United States and Canada
by Random House Distribution Services
1745 Broadway, New York, NY 10019
Tel: +1 (212) 572-2844   Fax: +1 (212) 572-4961
Inquiries: csorders@randomhouse.com

Series Editor Geoffrey Chesler
Design Bobby Birchall

Printed in Malaysia

Cover image: Old brick church in Gondar, Amhara.
©Carolyne/Dreamstime.com
The illustration on page 15 and the photograph on page 97 are reproduced by permission of the author.
Images on pages 41 © volff/fotolia.com; 51 © Mahesh Patil/fotolia.com; 108 © Kheng Guan Toh/fotolia.com.
Images on the following pages reproduced under Creative Commons License Attribution 2.0, 2.5, and 3.0: 13, 70, and 71 © Jialiang Gao; 18, 20, 80, 90, 112, and 136 © Steve Evans; 21 and 92 © Maurits V; 25 © Melka Kunture Museum; 28 and 64 © Ondrej Zvacek; 30 and 114 © Giustino; 31 (bottom) and 123 © Sam Effron; 32 © Oren neu dag; 50 © Manfred Werner-Tsui; 57 © Kolumbusjogger; 66 and 126 © Gyrofrog; 78 © Rama; 82 © Richard from Kansas City, United States; 99 © Niklas Schiffler; 104 © meg and rahul; 106 © Justin Clements; 107 © Badagnani; 111 © Thomas Faivre-Duboz; 113 © Lior Golgher; 117 © Tmanahan344; and 143 © Philip Kramer

About the Author

SARAH HOWARD is a botanical artist and writer who spent her childhood in Kenya. After graduating in African History and Social Anthropology from the School of Oriental and African Studies, University of London, in 1977, she became a journalist and researcher for two Anglican mission agencies, and undertook the archiving of the Leakey family papers in Kenya. After her marriage, she began commuting between Scotland and Ethiopia: in Scotland she runs a small business specializing in roasting Ethiopian coffees; in Ethiopia she is currently painting portraits of endemic plants. She helped illustrate the seminal *Flora of Ethiopia and Eritrea* (Addis Ababa University), and has written articles about the country for *Selamta*, the in-flight magazine of Ethiopian Airlines.

contents

contents

Map of Ethiopia

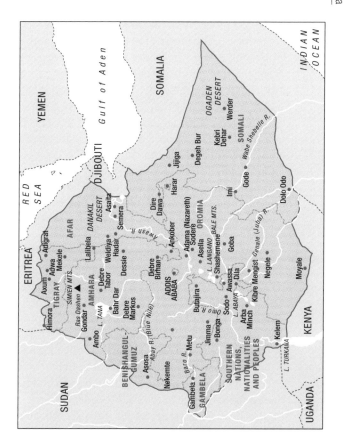

introduction

Set in Africa, but not wholly African; an isolated
nation, yet receptive to the outside world;
hierarchical and conservative, yet innovative and
desirous of modernity; conformist as a people, and
yet fiercely independent as individuals—the
Ethiopian identity defies definition. No sooner have
you made a generalisation than you realise it does
not apply to some other part of the country. This is
because Ethiopia was once an empire, made up of
many different peoples and cultures.

On the whole this book describes Ethiopia's
dominant culture, which is Orthodox Christian,
highland based, and uses Amharic as its first or
second language, and makes reference to other
regional cultures where it seems necessary.

Ethiopia exists simultaneously in different time
periods. It has a long documented history, and is
undergoing very great change. Its people, when they
see something new that might work to their
advantage, will embrace it and find ways to improve
on it. Modern democracy, however, has
understandably been slower to achieve given the
strong historical antecedents of its monarchy.

Then there is the question of urban and rural life.
Most Ethiopians live in the countryside, in much
the way their great grandparents did. City folk could
almost be another race. Their chic dress and skills
on the computer belong to the Western world; but
their prowess as horsemen, and skills as herbalists,
belong to the countryside. The book focuses mainly

on urban Ethiopians because they are the ones most likely to be encountered by foreigners. But, for perspective, everything we state should be tested against what rural people think or do.

All Ethiopians are proud of their history. They are so proud, in fact, that some outsiders see them as arrogant. They are, perversely, also almost proud of the fact that their country was not modernized as quickly as other African states with a colonial past: their freedom is worth more to them than having an infrastructure for economic development. Ethiopians are also passionate about bureaucracy. They feel no need to question it, although they can be masters of evasion, and bluff in the face of overbearing rule.

Outwardly formal and courteous, Ethiopians have a great sense of fun. They are witty and have a penchant for puns, and hugely enjoy slapstick.

Their courtesy is born of the consciousness of being members of a multilingual and multicultural polity, where in order to get on, people have to respect each other. When foreigners experience this, it is not because they are seen as superior (most Ethiopians believe they are in most respects superior to Westerners) but because they are being treated to the same politeness as an Ethiopian from a different region.

This book goes a short way toward introducing you to the Ethiopian peoples. Enjoy Ethiopia, and you will be warmly embraced by your hosts.

Key Facts

Official Name	Federal Democratic Republic of Ethiopia	The older name Abyssinia properly refers only to the Amhara and Tigray regions.
Capital City	Addis Ababa	Pop. 3.5 million (est.) Altitude 7,870 ft (2,400 m)
Administrative Regions and Capitals	Afar (Semera); Amhara (Bahr Dar); Benishangul-Gumuz (Asosa); Gambela (Gambela); Harar (Harar); Oromia (Addis Ababa); Somali (Jijiga); Southern Nations, Nationalities and Peoples (Awassa); Tigray (Mekele). Addis Ababa and Dire Dawa are chartered cities with the same status as the regions. Addis Ababa is the country's capital, capital of a region, and a chartered city.	
Official Federal Languages	Amharic is the official state language. English is the official foreign language.	Each region has its official language. Some use the Latin alphabet, others a script derived from the Ge'ez language.
Area	435,000 sq. miles (1.14 million sq. km)	
Borders	Eritrea, Djibouti, Somalia, Kenya, Sudan	
Climate	Temperate to alpine in the mountains; tropical in the lowlands. Varies with altitude and aspect	Two main seasons: dry from Oct. to May, and wet from June to Sept. Poss. "short rains" in March and April
Economy	Agriculture	Approx. 90% of people earn their living from the land.
Currency	Ethiopian Birr (ETB), divided into 100 Santim (centimes)	Coins of 1, 5, 10, 25, and 50 Santim; banknotes for 1, 5, 10, 50, and 100 Birr

Population	80 million. Half the population is under twenty.	Av. no. of children per woman: 5.4 Infant mortality: 61 per 1,000
Ethnic Makeup	Semitic (Amhara, Tigray, and Gurage), Cushitic (Oromo, Somali, and Afar), Nilotic (Nuer and Anuak)	There is a large pop. of Italians, Greeks, and Armenians, mostly in Addis Ababa.
Languages	There are 83 major languages and more than 200 dialects.	Amharinya and Tigrinya are the major Semitic langs.; Oromifa and Somali the main Cushitic langs.
Religion	Ethiopian Orthodox Christianity and Sunni Islam are the two major religions.	Also Protestant and Catholic Churches, and animistic beliefs in the south
Government	Democratically elected federal government, with elected regional governments	Local government consists of *woredas* (districts), town councils, and *kebeles* (parishes).
Electricity	220 volts, 50 Hz	Plugs are generally two-pronged.
Internet Domain	.et	
Telephone	Country code 251 Cell phone numbers within Ethiopia begin 09.	To call out of the country, dial 00 followed by the country code.
Calendar	The Ethiopian (Coptic) calendar used in addition to the Western (Gregorian) calendar	
Time Zone	GMT plus 3 hours, all year round	The Middle Eastern clock is also used in Ethiopia, and begins at sunrise, or 6:00 a.m.

chapter one

LAND & PEOPLE

GEOGRAPHY

Ethiopia rises from arid lowlands to lofty mountain towers: a landlocked country that sits on a well-watered mountain plateau in the Horn of Africa. Its lowlands border on Eritrea, Djibouti, and Somalia to the north and east; Kenya to the south; and Sudan to the west. This "island" in the middle of desert largely dictates Ethiopia's natural resources, human settlement, and history.

With its cooler temperatures the highland plateau, rising from 5,000 to 10,000 feet (1,500 to 3,000 meters), carries the bulk of the population, provides the best agricultural land, and can generate as much hydroelectricity as Ethiopia needs. Limits are, however, imposed by its rugged terrain. A complex structure of metamorphic, sedimentary, volcanic, and intrusive rocks is riven by a huge block fault averaging thirty miles wide (fifty kilometers) in the form of the Great Rift Valley. Smaller faults, particularly to the northwest of the Rift Valley, have created vast canyons, of which the Blue Nile gorge is the deepest. In the north the mountains rise to the peculiar, perpendicular-sided, flat-topped peaks of the Simien Mountains of more than 14,000 feet (4,300 meters). The highlands to the southeast of the Rift are gentler in character, but rise almost as high in the Bale Mountains, with the magnificent south-facing Harenna escarpment. The whole area continues to be unstable, with small earthquakes common, and hot springs prevalent.

Aptly described as "the reservoir of Africa," Ethiopia has river systems upon which its near neighbors in Somalia, Sudan, and Egypt are particularly reliant. Draining the northern mountains is the Abay (Blue Nile) River and its tributaries, which supply two-thirds of the Nile's water north of Khartoum. To the south, the Wabe Shebelle and Genale rivers flow to the Indian Ocean through Somalia. The Awash flows into desert near Djibouti, and the Omo flows into landlocked Lake Turkana. Many of these rivers are dammed to generate hydroelectricity.

The Rift Valley itself widens out in the north to the harsh Danakil desert, where the hottest annual mean temperature on earth has been recorded, and drops away in the south to the

desert of northern Kenya. In between, the altitude rises to about 5,500 feet (1,700 meters). A series of lakes along the Rift Valley floor provides irrigation where the water is fresh, though many are saline. From the plateau the land gives way to the Ogaden desert bordering Somalia in the east, and, to the west, humid lowlands bordering Sudan.

CLIMATE

Ethiopia's generally high altitude offsets the effects of its position in the tropics, just to the north of the Equator. Temperatures are cool at night and the main rains are usually very heavy. In the lowland fringes the climate can be uncertain and is a cause of food insecurity. The main rains (*kremt*) begin at the end of June in Addis Ababa, slightly later in Tigray, and peter out during September. Many foreigners choose this time to leave the country, but it is vital planting time for Ethiopian farmers. There is often a short rain (*belg*) about Easter when another planting is also possible. The southern part of the country is influenced by the monsoons blowing in from the Indian Ocean.

Temperatures vary with altitude. Ethiopians themselves refer to three zones: a cool zone (*dega*) in the highest mountains, where daytime temperatures range from freezing to 60°F (16°C) in the hot months; the temperate *weina dega* zone has temperatures from 60° to 86°F (16° to 30°C), and where a sweater is needed at night; and the *kolla* zone, lying below 5,000 feet (1,500 meters) in the deserts and at the bottoms of big river gorges, where daytime temperatures average 80°F (27°C).

FLORA AND FAUNA

Humans have modified greatly the natural
landscape in Ethiopia, particularly in the north.
Primary forests have been much reduced and the
Rift Valley is badly degraded. Yet there is much to
observe and to protect. As an "island" ecosystem,
Ethiopia has developed both a specialist natural
life, particularly in the highest and driest areas,
as well as a high degree of biodiversity, notably
in economically important food crops such as
cereals and coffee. A possible biodiversity hot
spot exists between southern Ethiopia through
to southern Arabia. The Rift Valley, with its lakes,
is an important migration route for birds, and a
number of national parks and reserves exist to
protect unique fauna.

The Australian eucalyptus tree (*Eucalyptus
globulus*) dominates the eye around Addis Ababa,
and every other town and village, and is an
essential source of fuel. It is, though, only one
among over 7,000 higher plant species existing in
Ethiopia, of which about 12 percent
are endemic. Vegetation zones
broadly follow Ethiopia's complex
topography. These range from
semidesert scrub, through
acacia woodland, to moist
montane forest—in which coffee
still grows wild—or dry montane
forest containing magnificent
trees, such as the *Podocarpus*
and the medicinally important
Hagenia abyssinica. Vivid red *Acanthus
sennii* grow along the roadsides in this zone,

a striking plant endemic to Ethiopia. High in the alpine regions, where nightly frosts are a feature, there are plants well adapted to their environment, such as prickly clumps of the shrub *Helichrysum*, and the giant treelike *Lobelia*, whose old leaves protect its stem from freezing.

The Rift Valley lakes provide an important migration corridor between Eastern Europe and Southern Africa and, as a result, Ethiopia, together with Eritrea, is one of Africa's hot spots for bird-watching. There are over 860 known species of birds, including 16 species endemic to Ethiopia, many of which are locally common and easy to spot. These include the Black-winged Lovebird (*Agapornis taranta*), found near water in cities, and the Thick-billed Raven (*Corvus crassirostris*) on the hills surrounding Addis Ababa.

Ethiopia is also home to 263 mammal species, of which there are 30 endemics. A number of national parks and conservation areas exist to protect these animals, but the pressures of a growing population and livestock make some of them difficult to sustain. The Abyssinian wolf (*Canis simensis*), easily seen in the Bale Mountains, with about four hundred in existence is the world's rarest canine.

Land degradation is one of the major conservation issues facing the government of Ethiopia, together with the protection of forests to preserve rainfall.

PEOPLE

The Ethiopians are a mixture of African and Middle Eastern peoples forming several distinctive nations and tribes. In the west, tall Nilotic tribes straddle the border with Sudan. In the south and east are various Cushitic-speaking peoples, such as the clannish cattle-rearing Oromo who have migrated northward into the area, and nomadic camel-keeping Somalis who straddle the southeast border. In the north are Semitic-speaking and sedentary Amharas and Tigrayans who define the Christian heartland.

Eighty different languages are spoken in the country with a great many more dialects. Amharic is the working language in Addis Ababa and is understood in most other parts of the country, since it was the language of education during the Marxist government of the Derg (1974–91). It has its own script that, like Arabic, uses a system of phonetic consonants with extra markings for the vowels but, unlike Arabic, is written from left to right. Its transliteration into English gives rise to various spellings that can and do confuse the outsider.

In more recent centuries, families from various European nationalities have made their way to Ethiopia and many of them have intermarried with Ethiopians. These include Greeks, Armenians, and Italians. A reverse migration has also occurred from the time of the Derg, when Ethiopians created their own diaspora—an estimated one million are living in the United States, and probably the same number again in Europe.

About two million people are added to the population each year, representing a 2.5 percent growth rate. Half the estimated population of 77 million is under twenty years old. With so many new mouths to feed each year, the government is presented with a formidable challenge to its development policy.

REGIONS
Tigray

This northernmost region covers the highlands in the northeast of Ethiopia. It encompasses the ancient Kingdom of Axum, and was divided in the nineteenth century into part of what is now highland Eritrea and that which remained part of Ethiopia. The Christian faith and the language, Tigrinya, are common bonds both within Tigray and with the Eritreans across the border. On the whole, its agricultural land has become badly degraded, but there are rich tourist opportunities in historical centers such as Axum and the many clusters of rock-hewn churches around Tigray. Mekele, founded by Yohannes IV in the late nineteenth century, is the capital.

Amhara

This region covers the Amharic-speaking provinces of Gondar, Gojjam, Wollo, and North Shoa in the central highlands of Ethiopia, north of the Rift Valley. Its people are mostly Christian, but there are many Muslims—especially in Wollo, which borders the Rift Valley where  Muslim camel traders mix with highlanders at the big markets at the foot of the escarpment. Small-scale farming is generally practiced. The leafy,

lakeside city of Bahr Dar by Lake Tana is capital of
Amhara. Other main towns are Dessie, in Wollo,
Gondar in the north, and various ancient sites
such as Ankober and Debre Markos.

Afar

The Afar language, Islam, and camels bind the
Afar Region, which covers the hot, arid lowlands
to the east of the highland plateau. The Awash
River flows through it providing the Afar region's
only crop-producing potential, although the water
never reaches the sea and peters out in a series of
saline lakes near the Djibouti border. It is bound
to its neighboring regions by trade and by nomads
who bring their camels to grasslands in the higher
areas during the dry season. The old capital,
Asaita, is the center of a relatively well-irrigated
area on the Awash River. The capital has moved
to the new town of Semera.

Harar

This is the smallest region and surrounds the
ancient walled city of Harar. Coffee and *chat* are
the mainstays of the economy. Most people are
Muslim, though there is one important Christian
pilgrimage center, Kulubi Mariam, near Harar.
Harar is an ancient Muslim site where a unique
language called Adare is spoken.

Dire Dawa

One of two chartered cities (along with Addis
Ababa), Dire Dawa lies northwest of Harar on
the Djibouti-Addis Ababa railway. It is Ethiopia's
second-largest city and a major industrial and

trading center. It has an airport and its inhabitants are cosmopolitan, in contrast to the surrounding mainly Somali people.

Somali Region
Peopled by ethnic Somalis and covering the Ogaden desert, the Somali Region is probably the least accessible to outsiders. All Muslim, mostly camel keeping, watered only by the Genale (Juba) and Wabe Shebelle rivers that rise in the Bale Mountains, the region borders on both the orderly semiautonomous Somaliland (formerly British Somaliland) and the disturbed area of Somalia (formerly Italian Somaliland), which gives Ethiopia its greatest security problem. Jijiga, to the east of Harar, is the main town.

Oromia
This is the largest of Ethiopia's regions and covers

all the various Oromo-speaking peoples, from Shoa in the north, to the Kenyan border in the south, and most of western Ethiopia, including Wellega. Addis Ababa is the capital, and it includes large towns such as Debre Zeit, Jimma, Adama (also known by its former name, Nazareth), and Asella. It includes the Bale Mountains and most of the eastern side of the Rift Valley. The Oromo language has diverse dialects and the people are largely Muslim or Christian, particularly of the Protestant kind. All types of agriculture are practiced, including nomadic cattle keeping in the Rift Valley, and sedentary agriculture in the highlands. There, the potential is high with rich volcanic and well-watered soils.

Southern Nations, Nationalities and Peoples (SNNP) Region

The sheer diversity of small linguistic groups, cultures, and religions makes this area difficult to generalize. It covers the highland area on the western side of the southern Rift Valley in the southwest of

Ethiopia, and includes important nations, such as: Gurage, centered on Butajira, in the Gurage Highlands; Welayta, centered on Sodo; Sidama, centered on Dila; as well as small tribes favoured by tourists, such as the Mursi, Hamer, and Konso. It also includes the coffee-bearing forests around the town of Bonga, which is reached via Jimma. Awassa, on Lake Awassa, is its capital and is gateway to the important coffee-growing Sidamo area to the south. This area, too, is agriculturally rich in coffee and cattle, with important forests on the higher slopes of the Rift Valley scarps. Its peoples practice a mixture of religions, including mainly Protestant and Catholic Christianity, Islam, and paganism. Amharic is the working language.

Gambela

Centered on the town of Gambela on the Baro River, Gambela Region is low-lying, humid, and hot. Its people are mainly a mixture of nomadic cattle-keeping Nuer and Anuak, a Nilo-Saharan language group, who straddle the border with southern Sudan. They are traditionally pagan, but recently there has been a surge of Protestant Christianity among them. The Baro River flows through Gambela, before becoming the Sobat in Sudan, and flowing into the White Nile. Gambela town was an important port trading with British Sudan.

Benishangul-Gumuz

This region to the northwest of Ethiopia, which straddles the Abay (Nile), was carved out of western Gojjam and northern Wellega. It is mostly highland, but dips down toward the Sudanese border. There are diverse peoples, ranging from the Berta, Gumuz, and Shinasha, who have more in common with the Sudanese, to large numbers of Amhara and Tigrayans, who were resettled during the Derg era, and Oromos. More than 60 percent of the land is forested, including bamboo, eucalyptus, and rubber and resin trees, which are important to the local economy. Asosa is the capital.

Addis Ababa

Addis Ababa is one of two chartered cities in Ethiopia with its own elected mayor and its own administrative structure. It is also the capital of the country, and by far the largest city, with more than three million people. It was founded in 1887 around hot springs, known as Finfinne, by Emperor

Menelik II. His wife, the Empress Taitu, who enjoyed the hot springs, gave the name Addis Ababa ("new flower" in Amharic) to the emergent town. When local supplies of wood began to be exhausted, it was the introduction of the eucalyptus tree in the 1890s that saved the capital from moving elsewhere.

Addis Ababa sprawls over several hills and ravines at a heady altitude ranging from 7,000 to 9,000 feet (2,100 to 2,700 meters) with little noticeable difference between affluent and shanty-type housing. Five major road arteries radiate from the city to the regions, with Meskel Square the heart of the city, where big national events take place. The city is completely surrounded by Oromia Region, and you'll notice you have crossed the border when you begin to see signs in the Oromo language using Latin letters. Since 2000, a frenzy of road building—divided highways, overpasses, and ring roads—has both eased movement as well as caused dire congestion, with traffic pouring around work zones, vying with pedestrians and, sometimes, their livestock.

The Mercato is a huge market area and forms a distinct community within the city. The proportion of Muslims is higher than elsewhere, and the various nationalities of Ethiopia mingle with long-established foreign communities, of which the Yemeni is by far the biggest. Trading and commerce in both traditional and new commodities, from hides and skins to laptop computers, is based on relationships of trust that sometimes go back several generations.

Easier for foreigners to manage when purchasing goods are either the many arcades springing up all over town, or the Piazza, another traditional commercial area.

Although areas of the city have traditional names, and there are some street signs, it is more usual to find your way about by means of local reference points, such as a church or an embassy.

A BRIEF HISTORY

The story of Ethiopia begins with the birth of humankind, and interplays with that of the Middle East. Nevertheless, its mountaintop position in Africa caused a unique Christian monarchy to develop in its heartland, providing the basis for a modern nation to adapt and change to twenty-first century norms.

The Cradle of Mankind

The story begins some 3.2 million years ago when humans were beginning to take shape. The discovery in 1974 of Dinkenesh (also known as "Lucy"), the oldest known hominid skeleton, in the Rift Valley at Hadar in Afar Region, seems to establish Ethiopia as the Cradle of Mankind. More recently, in 1992, bones were found, also in Afar, in sediment dated to 4.4 million years old. These seem to be a "missing link" between hominids and their immediate ancestors—these bones were named *Ardipithecus ramidus*. Shortly afterward, man-made stone tools dating to between 2.6 to 2.5 million years old were found both in Afar and in the Omo Valley sections of the Rift Valley. These early hominids are assumed to have migrated northward and eastward initially, and to have established other populations from which modern racial groupings have been formed. Perhaps the name given by Ethiopians for the Blue Nile—Ghion, also used in the Bible's Book of Genesis for one of the four rivers of Eden—reflects this earliest of early times?

Ethiopia's antiquity is also revealed by numerous rock paintings throughout the country, some as old as 10,000 years. Although harder to date, Ethiopia is also known to be a major center of plant domestication and crop diversity: the staple grain *teff*, as well as the oilseed *nug*, finger millet, *chat*, and coffee, whether imported or native, have sufficient unique variations to indicate a very long history of cultivated farming in the area.

In the annals of documented history from Egypt, mention is made of goods being sent from an area of Ethiopia to the Pharaohs, in about 3500 BCE. This area in the southern Red Sea, known as the Land of Punt, rich in myrrh, gold, ivory, and slaves, might be Tigray. The Book of Kings in the Bible makes reference to the land of Ophir, with similar trade goods. The Greek Ptolemys, rulers of Egypt from the early fourth century BCE, specifically mention in their writings the port of Adulis, very close to present-day Massawa in Eritrea. By that time Ethiopia was well-known to the Greeks, who had given it its name, meaning "the Land of Burned Faces."

Signs of the first civilization in the area appeared halfway through the first millennium BCE. The stone palaces and buildings at Yeha, twenty miles north of Axum, along with numerous other sites, reveal a rich culture very similar to that in Saba, southern Arabia, in their religion, language, and architecture.

By 300 BCE the Kingdom of Axum was born—a rich trading nation with a foot on both sides of the Red Sea, routes to Egypt both inland and by the Red Sea, and trails to the south, where valuable commodities could be obtained. The Axumites spoke a Semitic language similar to the liturgical language of Ge'ez, which they originally wrote in a Sabaean script; they worshipped many gods with Sabaean names, also identified with Greek gods; and they minted coins. They built impressive stone palaces, and erected tall stone stelae (pillars, or vertical tablets)—one of them, at 520 tons and 108 feet (33 meters) high, is the largest stone object known to have been worked by men.

Modern Beginnings in Axum

Modern Ethiopia is based on this Kingdom of
Axum when, under King Ezana, it embraced the
Christian Gospel in about 330 CE. On Ezana's
coins, and in inscriptions around town, pagan gods
were replaced by the Christian Cross. Ezana
determined not
only Ethiopia's
dominant religion
today, but also the
region's dominant
Semitic languages,
its literacy, and its
continued links
with the eastern
Mediterranean.
Despite the
Kingdom of

Axum's decline in the eighth century, when the rise
of Islamic trade isolated Ethiopia, the hallmarks of
the period remain to this day.

The Rise of a Feudal Nation: the Medieval Period

Ethiopia emerged from undocumented obscurity
early in the second millennium as an advanced
feudal nation. Its empires and kingdoms waxed and
waned during the subsequent thousand years largely
unnoticed by Western Europe, sometimes based in
Tigray, sometimes further west, sometimes further
south in Shoa. The feudal model was a means of
organizing the country and providing soldiers for
war, all centered on an elaborate and sophisticated
royal court. Western Europeans only became
conscious of Ethiopia during the Crusades, when it

was seen as an ally against the Muslims. The legend of Prester John, the ruler of a Christian kingdom surrounded by Muslims, arose in Europe in the mid-twelfth century.

From Axum, power shifted south to Lasta where the monarchs of the Zagwe Dynasty (1150–1270) established their rule. They left no literature, but their high point was the creation of the Lalibela rock churches, built to represent Jerusalem. They ruled as descendants of King Solomon of Israel, a status made potent by the gifting to Ethiopia of the Deir es-Sultan monastery in Jerusalem.

The Solomonic succession became justified in the apocryphal fourteenth-century *Kebra Negast* (*Book of the Glory of Kings*), a document that tells the Ethiopian version of the story of the Queen of Sheba's visit to Jerusalem to witness Solomon's riches. The story augments the Bible's version, with an account of how Solomon tricked the Queen into

his bed. When she returned home she gave birth to a son, who became the Emperor Menelik I. It also adds the rider of how the Ark of the Covenant, which housed the stone tablets given by God to Moses, which was kept in Solomon's temple in Jerusalem, was removed by Menelik and taken down the Nile for safekeeping in Ethiopia. Today, these tablets are closely guarded in the Church of St. Mary of Zion in Axum, and their authenticity is impossible to verify.

This was indeed a Christian society, with strong Judaist elements, in which scholars flourished and literacy was nurtured in monasteries. Pilgrimage to Jerusalem increased contact with Europeans. A diplomatic mission of thirty men was sent from Ethiopia to Spain and Rome in the early fourteenth century, and later, in the 1390s, a Florentine trader appeared in Ethiopia. The martial arts were highly respected as aristocrats all over the country, jostling for influence at court, were expected to support the emperor's wars. The series of dynasties that ruled during these centuries owed their survival, or not, to leaders with extraordinary political skill and military prowess both within the area and against any common enemies without.

Defending Ethiopia's Christian Heritage

By the sixteenth century Ethiopia's trading rivalry with its Muslim neighbors was the torch that nearly led to defeat for the Christian descendants of Axum. The most successful Muslim commander was Mohammed Gragn ("the Left-Handed"), from the Emirate of Adal in the lowlands. He had access to superior arms from the Ottomans, and waged a *jihad* ("holy war"), defeating Emperor Lebna Dengel in 1529, and continuing to overrun most of eastern and southern Ethiopia. Christian Ethiopia was saved by the assistance of the Portuguese, known to the Ethiopians from an earlier diplomatic mission, who were the Ottomans' main rivals on the East African coast. Mohammed Gragn was finally defeated in 1541.

At the same time, a migration of Cushitic-speaking and pagan Oromo clans was moving northward to settle widely in the highlands. They added another dimension to Ethiopia's political and demographic mix, and have entirely changed the ethnic makeup of southern and eastern Ethiopia.

In 1557, Jesuit missionaries from Portugal arrived. They set up missions with ornate churches and buildings, still seen near Lake Tana, but they were summarily expelled by Emperor Fasilidas in 1632, following a miscalculated conversion to Catholicism by his predecessor, and foreigners were then barred from entering the country. However, from the beginning of the eighteenth century until the rise of Emperor Tewodros, there followed, in biblical terminology, a chaotic "Time of the Judges" (*mesafent)*, caused by internal infighting, which weakened the central authority of the emperors.

The Nineteenth Century and the Beginnings of Modernization

A semblance of order arrived with a brilliant warlord from the west, who was crowned Emperor Tewodros in 1855. He offered a sense of national unity and marked out a process of military, land, and Church reform. The Emperor built up a good rapport with certain foreigners, but, tragically, he suffered from manic depression and paranoia and eventually took his own life at Maqdala, in 1868, when British troops were sent to rescue a number of foreigners held hostage by him on a mountaintop.

By now Ethiopia was being drawn willingly, or unwillingly, into international affairs by the march of European and Ottoman imperialism, and by its

own need for guns and other supplies. Tewodros's Tigrayan successor, Yohannes IV, was killed by Sudanese Mahdists at Galabat in 1889, which gave the Shoan king from the south the opportunity to seize his chance. He was crowned Emperor Menelik II (the first Menelik had been the son of Solomon of Israel). His first major confrontation was with the Italians, then in control of present-day Eritrea and keen to expand into Ethiopia. At the Battle of Adwa in 1896, Menelik's victory against the better armed, but numerically inferior, European force had a palpable effect on both sides. Menelik then turned his attention to expansion, pushing the limits of his authority southward, westward, and eastward, until he came up against the territorial ambitions of the French and the British colonial powers then in present-day Djibouti, Somalia, and Kenya.

His empire secured, Menelik II was now able to devote time to serious modernization of the

country. He replaced Ankober with a new capital, Addis Ababa, on the southernmost edge of Christian Ethiopia, now more or less the center of the country. Like rulers before and after him, Menelik took care in choosing European advisers, trying not to be too reliant on any one nation. He was devoted in particular to his Swiss adviser, Alfred Ilg, but he also used the French to build a railway and print the first postage stamps, the Russians to build the first hospital, the Italians the first road in Addis Ababa, and the British a bank.

Emperor Haile Selassie, Ethiopia's Last Monarch
Haile Selassie's rise to power in the early twentieth century was, like that of his predecessors, paved with blood. After Menelik II's death in 1913, there followed the stumbling rule for a few years by his grandson, Iyasu, who was deposed in 1916. Menelik's daughter, Zauditu, was then proclaimed

Empress, though real power lay with a cousin, Ras Teferi, who was made Regent. He had won a battle against Iyasu's father, Mikael, at Sagale in 1916, thereby gaining the foothold he needed. He was intelligent, able, and familiar with the outside world, having been educated in a modern French school in Ethiopia. He was eventually crowned Emperor Haile Selassie in 1930.

Ras Teferi instigated another burst of progressive projects, again with the help of a medley of foreign advisers. He employed White Russians to train his army, he outlawed slavery, and, in 1923, took Ethiopia into the League of Nations. Progress was halted when the Italians, avenging Adwa, mounted a brutal campaign in 1935 to occupy Ethiopia.

Following Italy's entry into the Second World War, a combination of British Commonwealth and Ethiopian Patriot forces attacked the Italians from all sides and routed them in 1941. Emperor Haile Selassie made a triumphal entry into his

capital on May 5, the day he had lost it five years earlier. He then had to reestablish his authority, first making it clear to the British that he was the rightful ruler, and then to his own people, the ruler of Gojjam being particularly vexing to him. Tragically, most of the Western-educated elite had either been murdered or had gone into exile, making it more difficult to resume the process of modernization. In his foreign relations he became closer to the USA and other Western nations during the Cold War.

Increasingly, however, Haile Selassie failed to balance traditional forces with the new intelligentsia and their links with the Communist world. Following an attempted coup in 1960, an expensive war with Somalia over the Ogaden region in 1964, and a famine in 1972, he was deposed by radical elements in the armed forces in 1974.

A Thorn in Ethiopia's Side: Eritrea
Eritrea is both Ethiopia's closest neighbor and its most bitter enemy. It is part of the same highland plateau, its people are largely part of the same Tigrinya-speaking Christian stock, eating the same food and wearing the same clothes, and yet coexisting as separate nations has proved troublesome to both sides.

Eritrea was formed out of an area that came under Italian suzerainty in the late nineteenth century. During what was known as Europe's "Scramble for Africa," the Italians occupied parts of the Red Sea coast in present-day Eritrea. Under the 1889 Treaty of Wuchale, Emperor Menelik recognized the Italians' influence over the local rulers of this part of the hinterland, in return for Italian recognition of his sovereignty further south. However, the Italians misinterpreted the Treaty, pressed on further and occupied Adwa and Mekele, followed by Axum and Adigrat later. Greatly provoked, Menelik sent his army to Adwa in 1896 and inflicted a heavy defeat on the larger and better equipped Italian army. In the subsequent peace terms Eritrea became an Italian colony and Ethiopia retained its independence.

In 1935, however, the Italians avenged Adwa by using Eritrea (and Italian Somaliland, centered on Mogadishu) as a base to invade Ethiopia using many "colonial" troops from Eritrea. Despite Ethiopia's internationally

recognized independence and membership in the League of Nations, the Italians drove their army southward, using illegal mustard gas in the process, and took Addis Ababa on May 5, 1936. Emperor Haile Selassie was persuaded to go into exile in Britain while many of his people fought from within, and suffered badly as a result.

While Italy tried to turn Addis Ababa into the capital of Italian East Africa (*Africa Orientale Italiana*) in the Horn of Africa—building excellent roads that radiated from the city toward Asmara, in Eritrea, in the north, and to Mogadishu, in the Italian colony of Somalia, to the south, and importing Italian peasant farmers to colonize the best land—they never managed to achieve a *pax Italiana* in the country as a whole.

The end to the short-lived colony came with the Italian defeat in 1941, and British Military Administrations were set up in all former Italian colonies. Ethiopia quickly reestablished its independence, but in Eritrea and Somalia the problems were different.

Eritrea's future was determined by an international commission in 1947, consisting of France, the UK, the USA, and the USSR. They found three quite different views: mainly Christians who favored union with Ethiopia; mainly Muslims who were against union; and mainly ex-Italian colonists who were, naturally, pro-Italy. The conundrum was handed to the United Nations in 1948, which passed a controversial resolution making Eritrea a partner in an Ethiopian-dominated federation. Many Ethiopians moved north to Asmara and intermarried, and many Eritreans moved south and intermarried with Ethiopians.

The arrangement was never happy, however, and in 1961 the Eritreans made their first bid for real independence under various Christian and Muslim groups (later coalescing under the Eritrean Peoples Liberation Front (EPLF)). Ethiopia found it had the pretext it needed, and forcibly brought Eritrea under direct sovereignty. This led to persistent war for the next thirty or so years, first against Haile Selassie, and, after 1974, against the Ethiopian Derg leader, Mengistu Haile Mariam. Both sides were aided and abetted by the bigger antagonists of the Cold War. When the Russians abandoned

Mengistu, after the fall of the Berlin Wall in 1989, the EPLF took Massawa. It then combined with the mainly Tigrayan Ethiopian Peoples' Revolutionary Democratic Front (EPRDF) under Meles Zenawi, and, in 1991, marched into Addis Ababa. In 1993, after a referendum, Eritrea became a sovereign nation, with, seemingly, a sympathetic neighbor in Ethiopia.

Differences between them, however, soon became apparent and, in 1998, they exploded over a disputed boundary in a poorly populated and infertile piece of land. Bitter trench warfare was conducted for two years, thousands of lives were lost on both sides, and their respective treasuries were drained to pay for arms. A peace accord was achieved in 2000, but the truce is deeply fragile as a boundary commission attempts to reconcile the two countries' interests. Meanwhile, the border is closed leaving a simmering atmosphere and families divided.

Marxist Rule (1974–91)

After Haile Selassie's overthrow, Mengistu Haile Mariam, emerged as leader of the Marxist Provisional Military Administrative Council, known as the Derg, in 1977. He ruled for fourteen years until he himself was deposed in 1991. Opposition to the Derg was immediate. The intelligentsia took to the streets and, in the Derg crackdown known as the Red Terror, 100,000 people died. Yet again, educated Ethiopians were either eliminated or went into exile.

Opposition to Derg rule also grew within the provinces: the Oromo, Tigrayans, and Somalis in

Ogaden all took their cue and mounted nationalist campaigns. Dissatisfaction was fed by the central government's stranglehold on the economy and the resultant shortage of food, by an unpopular resettlement program, and by a disastrous drought in Wollo and Tigray in 1984–85. After months of tension, when Ethiopians scrambled to get out of the country, and war fronts on every road made it impossible to travel around freely, the end came in May 1991. Meles Zenawi's EPRDF tanks, supported by the Eritrean EPLF and backed by the USA, rumbled into Addis Ababa, past jubilant crowds along the Jimma Road by the old airport, which only days before had seen Mengistu's helicopters taking off in daily droves in an attempt to stem the EPRDF advance.

The only generally recognized contribution to Ethiopia's development made by the Derg, with its socialist ideals, was to extend primary schooling for children, and to release the peasantry from their subservience to the aristocracy. For the first time this class of people had a voice through the *kebele* (local council) system that had been set up throughout the country, and that still exists today.

GOVERNMENT AND POLITICS

Meles's government immediately revised the constitution, and set about balancing the power of Ethiopia's main nations, or tribes, by devolving government and forming self-governing regions under a federal system, and by trying to make up ground lost in the Derg years. Two general elections have been held, but the bitter war with Eritrea, 1998–2000, cast a shadow over the early years. Since then, despite some progress, economic development has been a tough challenge in the face of a fast-rising population and the ups and downs of a global free market.

However, the art of governing Ethiopia has always been to balance a centralized autocracy with regional devolution. It has never been easy to unify the country and please its parts. The current ruling party is dominated by Tigrayans, in power for the first time since the reign of Yohannes IV, and who were the main antagonists of Mengistu's Amhara-led government. Deep suspicion prevails, particularly among the Amhara and Oromo, as to the government's real interest in the development of the country as a whole.

The disputed general election in 2005 saw a record number of voters—90 percent of the

electorate turned out. It saw Meles Zenawi retaining his post as prime minister, and his party keeping its majority in parliament. The main opposition party, the Coalition for Unity and Democracy (CUD), which meanwhile increased the number of its seats, and won a huge majority in Addis Ababa, declined to take its seats on the grounds of alleged electoral fraud. Rioting broke out in June, and again in November 2005, which was violently suppressed. In the next election, in 2010, the EPRDF won a landslide victory, but Meles Zenawi died in office in 2012 and was replaced by his deputy Hailemariam Desalegn.

Despite these political setbacks the EPRDF has set in motion a hugely ambitious development program to build up Ethiopia's infrastructure, building roads, schools, and clinics across the country.

A new constitution gives Parliament two chambers: the larger is the Council of People's Representatives, with 547 constituency members elected for five-year terms; and the Council of the Federation, which has 110 members drawn from the regions. The president is elected, by a joint session of both houses of Parliament, for six years, and the prime minister is elected by the majority in the House of People's Representatives.

For administrative purposes the country is divided into the nine ethnically based regions and two chartered cities. At the local level the regions are divided hierarchically into zones, *woredas* and *kebeles* (local community councils).

The judiciary is officially independent, and administered by the Ministry of Justice. The president of the Federal Supreme Court is recommended by the prime minister and appointed by the House of People's Representatives. The law is based on the Napoleonic Code, but incorporates aspects of traditional Ethiopian law.

Relations with China and India are strongly encouraged by the EPRDF. Tensions with Eritrea may be more easily resolved by Meles Zenawi's successor. Ethiopia supported the official, if contested, government of neighboring Somalia militarily until early 2009. Ethiopia also maintains close relationships with the internationally unrecognized republic of Somaliland (a former British colony based in Hargeisa, in northern Somalia), with Djibouti, and with Sudan.

THE ECONOMY

The economy is essentially in transition between a Marxist command model and a liberal capitalist one.

All agricultural land was nationalized in 1975 and remains as such, but farmers have usufruct rights. Foreigners and local investors can now lease land for periods up to forty years, depending on the region. The main utilities, such as the electric power corporation, telecommunications and airlines, and the largest banks, remain state owned. A commodities exchange was inaugurated in 2008, but there is no stock exchange as yet.

Agriculture is the mainstay of the economy, and the EPRDF's development policy is agriculture-led. Most people live off the land (90 percent), most exports are agricultural (60 percent), and agriculture accounts for nearly half of GDP—this despite frequent droughts, rising population, and a heritage of land tenure that has militated against good farming or cash production. The main products are cereals, pulses, coffee, oilseed, cotton, sugarcane, *chat*, cut flowers, hides, cattle, sheep, goats, and fish, of which coffee, *chat*, live cattle, hides, and oilseeds are exported.

Coffee is mostly channeled through the government's newly established Commodity Exchange in Addis Ababa, though organic and Fairtrade coffees bypass this system. The dominant coffee traders are mainly Muslims with their contacts across the Red Sea, and Dire Dawa is a major hub for this trade.

Ethiopia has the potential to produce 30,000 megawatts of electricity (enough for the country's need and for export), mostly from hydroelectric schemes on the Abay, the Omo, and the Awash rivers. Most people, however, rely on eucalyptus wood for their cooking needs, and industry uses very little electricity, so the source is little exploited. Almost all oil is imported via Sudan and Djibouti, but 5 percent of all gasoline is ethanol and jatropha is grown to provide biodiesel. There is potential to produce more biofuels, particularly from molasses.

Gold is the most valuable mineral in Ethiopia, although there are large reserves of lower value, cement-related, industrial minerals that are of high quality. The search for, and exploitation of, other minerals continues.

Traditional village and town markets operate in the regions, and a large flow of hard currency comes through remittances from expatriate Ethiopians in America and Europe.

INTERNATIONAL RELATIONS

Ethiopians have always tried to balance foreign influences to their advantage. This means they maintain close relations with Israel as well as with Arab countries, and with China and Russia, as well as with the USA and the European Union. Addis Ababa is the diplomatic center of Africa,

with the headquarters of the African Union in the city, and every African country maintaining a diplomatic mission there. The United Nations' Economic Commission for Africa (ECA) is housed in an historic multistory block off Meskel Square.

chapter two

VALUES & ATTITUDES

NATIONAL IDENTITY

Modern Ethiopia is the product of a long history, an ancient kingdom, peopled by a mixture of Semitic and Cushitic races, living in the fastness of the high mountain plateaus in the Horn of Africa. Once an empire, today it is a federation of nations with a distinctive common culture that embraces and holds together several greater and lesser regional subcultures.

Since their conversion to Christianity in the fourth century, Ethiopians have shared a tradition of law and moral philosophy based on books written in Geʿez, their ancient common language, with its unique script, still used in churches today. Later, their country was cut off from the rest of Christendom by the rise of Islam, becoming a religious and cultural island with a strong feudal and monarchical tradition.

When the empire expanded to the south, west, and east of its historic core in the nineteenth century, it brought into the Ethiopian fold Muslim and pagan cultures and peoples, with Protestant and Catholic Christianity added to the mix. Rapid modernization in the twentieth century, with its attendant Western democratic values, contributed to an already rich culture.

So what is *Ityopyawinet*, the Amharic word for the distinct quality of being Ethiopian? Ethiopians find it easy to recognize and hard to define. They admire and practice the virtues of humility, politeness, and patience, and yet they can be extraordinarily anarchic drivers and fierce warriors. They are proud of their culture, are hospitable to guests and strangers, and yet allow foreigners to be hassled by beggars and children. Ethiopians value long friendships, have difficulty sustaining extended family life, with divorce and remarriage common, and they have a deeply pessimistic view of human nature.

Red in Tooth and Claw

"The eye of the leopard is on the goat, and the eye of the goat is on the leaf."

Ethiopian proverb

They are seldom surprised by betrayal, and can maintain personal feuds for decades. They are often individualistic rather than team players, methodical rather than intuitive, intellectual rather than creative.

ETHIOPIA'S CULTURES
Amhara
The Amhara possess great political acumen and protect their corner with considerable cunning. They are the traditional ruling class, proud and impulsive, and the speakers of Ethiopia's subtle and complex national language, Amharic, with its own script.

What's in a Name?

Amhara personal names are often expressive of aspirations to mastery: *Asselefech* ("she made them line up"), *Asfa Wossen* ("expand the borders"), *Mulugeta* ("master of all"), and, indeed, *Muluimabet* "mistress of all."

Amharic is susceptible of ambiguity to a remarkable degree, and Amharas have a tradition of writing clever, short poems, with an overt meaning and a hidden meaning, referred to as "wax and gold."

Gurage

Gurage people are traders and know the value of money. They are not easily cheated, and dominate much of Addis Ababa's shopkeeping. Guragues eat a food made out of a false banana tree called *enset*, which few other Ethiopians eat. They also dominate the vegetable growing sector. Guragues speak a Semitic language, and trace their origins to Gura, a district now in Eritrea.

Oromo

The Oromo people are hardworking, loyal, and great lovers of horses. They now form Ethiopia's largest nation, though some Oromo more easily identify with smaller cultural subunits. They pride themselves on a system of egalitarian ethics known as *gada*, and on their tradition of consensus and democracy. Their language has many dialects and has recently enjoyed a renaissance, now being used throughout the state of Oromia, and written in the Latin alphabet.

Tigray

Tigrayans see their land as the very cradle of Ethiopian Christianity and civilization, and tend to give their children names that reflect this; "Servant of Mary" (*Gabre Mariam*), and "Power of the Trinity" (*Haile Selassie*). Tigrayans historically have survived by skillful management of their relations with the other Ethiopian peoples. Their language is the closest descendant of ancient Ge'ez, and carries over the border into highland Eritrea, and their territory includes Axum, the oldest city in Ethiopia and its ecclesiastical capital.

Other Peoples

Added to the contemporary mix are Somalis, Afars, and Muslim Aderes, who have a tradition of government by sultans, or chiefs. Gambella and Beni Shangul peoples, and a multitude of smaller Southern and Western peoples, tend to be nonhierarchical, animistic and tribal, and belong to Nilotic or Omotic racial groups.

ATTITUDES TOWARD FOREIGNERS

White foreigners are commonly, and often affectionately, called *ferenj*, an Arabic word meaning "Frankish." There is some uncertainty whether white people who are also Orthodox Christians should be classed as *ferenj*; Asians, other Africans, and Arabs are definitely not classified in this way. Ethiopians enjoy the company of foreigners, and in the past notable foreigners have been guests at the invitation of rulers who tapped them for their knowledge.

Greeks, Italians, and Armenians who have married Ethiopians, or who are of mixed race and speak fluent Amharic, are scarcely treated as foreigners at all.

Short-term foreigners, diplomats, and tourists on the other hand, are often regarded as fair game to be exploited, sometimes subtly, often not. The areas around Addis Ababa's big hotels are notorious for *ferenji* hustlers, people who attach themselves ruthlessly to foreigners at the main door or gate, and will not let them go until they have obtained some gift or favor from them. Most Ethiopians deplore such hangers-on, but few steps are taken to solve or minimize the problem.

ATTITUDES TOWARD THEIR NEIGHBORS

Ethiopia's borders have been, for the most part, permeable and undemarcated. To the east, Somalis of the states of Djibouti, Somaliland, and Somalia interact constantly with the Somali region of Ethiopia, whose inhabitants form 6 percent of the Ethiopian population. There is usually one Somali in the Ethiopian cabinet. Somalis are not therefore a foreign people to Ethiopia, and there are many thousands of Somalis resident in Addis Ababa.

In the same way, the Nuer and Anuak peoples of Southern Sudan also form the core population of the Gambella region of Ethiopia. They are found in large numbers in Addis Ababa, are seen as different, but are not deemed foreign.

Kenya to the south is thought of as a friendly neighboring state, and although Borana and

Somali people, who are common to both countries, straddle the border, it is recognized that the Kenyan heartland is culturally different. Indeed, Ethiopians see themselves as being so distinct from the rest of Africa to the south that they can appear somewhat aloof.

Finally, Eritrea to the north is currently both the closest and the most hostile of Ethiopia's neighbors.

Once part of Ethiopia's borderlands, colonized by Italy, and then unhappily "reunited with the motherland" from 1951 to 1991, Eritrea shares a culture, a Christian Church, a cuisine, and a common language with Tigray in Ethiopia. Many thousands of Eritreans continue to live in Ethiopia, and there are still Ethiopians of Eritrean parentage in senior roles in the Ethiopian government. The presently disputed, closed, and fortified border, the cause of a costly war fought from 1998 to 2000, following on from a forty-year struggle for Eritrean independence, is a symbol of a tragic history that has divided families and wasted countless lives and resources.

RELIGIOUS TRADITION AND MODERN ASPIRATION

There has always been a tension in Ethiopian culture between conservative religious values and the aspiration to be *zemenawi,* or "modern." Many people are very devout, and others are tolerant and respectful of religion. Both the Orthodox and Muslim faiths have formed the Ethiopian character, which is patient, fatalistic, and long-suffering.

Nevertheless, the long-standing and deep-seated belief in modernization, particularly by its rulers, is coupled with the faint suspicion that Churches and Mosques have been obstacles in the path of this.

Ethiopians often long to live abroad, to get an education there, and so liberate themselves from

their homeland, and better themselves. During the monarchy, young intellectuals went abroad and returned home resolved to be begetters of change and agents of modernization. Nowadays, many seek to join relatives in settling permanently in the main cities of the Western world, particularly in North America, where they form distinct communities.

This new diaspora is itself influential in the homeland in many ways, both as an object of envy and admiration to those who have stayed back home, and as a major source of remittance income, which also supports opposition politicians. Back home, Westernization has brought about both a confident materialism and a rapid growth in Protestant Christianity.

EDUCATION

Ethiopians have always set a high value on education. Once the preserve of the Orthodox Church, literacy has now spread far and wide across the country. Indeed, one of the generally recognized successes of the Derg government was to improve substantially the literacy level of the population. Traditionally, education—as in the ability to speak, read, and write Amharic—led to a secure place in government service, and a status in society. Higher education continues to provide the means to an influential job today. Accordingly, the state is providing schools, colleges, and universities in all the major towns, though people make huge sacrifices to provide a private education for their children, to spare them the overcrowded "shift system," and give them an edge in the English language. Many graduates today still find their way into government service.

HIERARCHY AND ADMINISTRATION

Northern Ethiopians in particular are deeply conscious of hierarchy, a system with centuries of refinement. Government offices of all kinds, up and down the land, and in the remotest outposts, will house a group of very competent and efficient bureaucrats, often operating out of meager buildings. These offices are subject to frequent reorganization, but are always run hierarchically, with the big person at the top seated behind a large desk, and a table placed lengthwise in front of it with six to eight chairs along each side. He or she may be protected by a secretary, who controls entry to the big person's office—but there is a general presumption that anybody has access to these offices, and to the people at the top.

The administration, likewise, is organized hierarchically, with the country divided into regions, the regions divided into zones, the zones divided into *woredas*, and the *woredas* divided into *kebeles*. Officials will enforce policies at appropriate levels; requests will be passed up the hierarchy, and orders will be passed down.

MILITARISM

Militarism is a traditional virtue and carries respect in Ethiopia. Power has almost always been gained militarily, and the present regime is no exception. Many impartial Ethiopians see the use of force to control dissenters and disaffected groups as a necessity. Many Ethiopians used to carry guns as a matter of pride. With a natural tendency to hierarchy, and a need to place oneself under the protection of a powerful patron, the obligation to bear and use arms was always unquestioned in the feudal era. Nowadays, there is a core professional standing army and air force, and pacifism is unheard of. Few doubted the rightness of going to war in 1998 when Ethiopia's integrity was at stake, and recruitment among poor, rural young men was not a problem. Today there is no national service and no conscription, but the armed forces are adequately manned. Readiness to fight to protect the country's freedoms, and its national territory, remains part of Ethiopia's national psyche.

DEMOCRACY AND HUMAN RIGHTS

Ethiopia is nearer to being a democracy today than ever before in its history, but it is a country in transition—from a deeply autocratic past, to a federal parliamentary republic with a ceremonial head of state. There is, therefore, ambiguity about the commitment of government to real choice. Elections are held regularly, but few believe that the opposition parties will ever be "allowed" to win a general election. The disputed elections in 2005 seemed to reflect the historical tendency of the ruling elite to hold fast to power while preserving the outward formalities of democracy. Indeed, it is instructive, when searching for clues as to where real decision making takes place, to look beyond the usual instruments of democracy, such as parliament and the judicial system, and be aware that much happens behind the scenes. This political approach is particularly entrenched in Ethiopia, where so many are economically insecure, making a connection between one's job, and links with the ruling party, especially pertinent.

The Power of Patronage
"Whatever shines is the Sun, and whoever rules is our King."

Tigrinya proverb

Parliament, and the city and regional assemblies, do meet nonetheless, government is criticized, and newspapers express a variety of political views. Today, these newspapers are largely self-censored. If they overstep the mark, they may be closed down and their editors and journalists arrested.

Individual human rights have traditionally not figured highly on the national agenda. People can be locked away for years on suspicion of fraud and malpractice, and then cleared and released without compensation. Others undergo very long trials in court, with endless adjournments. Few Ethiopians seem to resent this; indeed, many would argue the need to control dissent.

It is fair to say that in modern Ethiopia if politics is avoided, and there is no involvement in fraud or major crime, neither the police nor the security services will be a problem. During the era of the Derg dictatorship this was not true. In those days active conformity was required; nonconformity was treated as a crime. There was active suppression of religion, and it was very hard to leave the country. Today, in matters of faith people are free to worship as they please, and anyone may obtain a passport and leave the country at will.

It is worth mentioning that the involvement of foreigners in political or human rights cases or causes is not tolerated. If you do choose to get involved you will probably be expelled from the country. A new law was passed in January 2009 preventing foreign charities, or local charities funded from abroad, from engaging in such activities.

ATTITUDES TO THE ENVIRONMENT

Although many parks and reserves exist, including the oldest conserved forest in Africa, set up by Emperor Zara Yakob in the fifteenth century, Ethiopia has not gone to great lengths to protect its wildlife.

However, Orthodox Ethiopians, unlike other Africans, have religious taboos against eating certain animals that are similar to Jewish taboos. Hence, wild duck and antelope are avoided, as are pigs and camels among domestic animals. It is also the case that copses of indigenous trees will be found around churches whereas they will have been cut down elsewhere. In southern areas, the Oromo people have a particular feeling for trees, particularly the wide canopy of the wild fig, known as *oda*, which provides such good shade, and trees will be found dotted around the area where they live.

In a system where so much manpower was, and continues, to be taken up with military activity, conservation of natural resources has taken a backseat. In addition, the burgeoning population needs to eat, and inroads are made into unprotected forest and land, not by speculators, but by small peasant farmers. Despite this there is a determined attempt to preserve and plant trees wherever possible.

Domestic animals, such as dogs, donkeys, mules, and horses, are treated as functionaries, and poverty will often prevent them from being fed properly or seen by a vet. However, Ethiopians can be sentimental and reluctant to kill an animal to put it out of its misery.

Addis Ababa still has an inadequate waste disposal system, and its citizens will tolerate mounds of trash in the streets, the pollution of rivers and the atmosphere by exhaust fumes, and will use open spaces as public toilets. There is a growing awareness of public aesthetics, however, and notable individuals are taking an interest in creating beautiful gardens and in clearing up the worst of the mess.

ATTITUDES TO PAIN AND SUFFERING
The approach to pain and suffering is one of stoicism and fatalism. If God will not remove it, you need to bear it.

There are evidently many poor people in Ethiopia. Their condition is more extreme in the cities where family ties may be lacking. Traditionally, begging outside church gates provided a form of social security—begging is in no way shameful. Indeed, supplication is done throughout all levels of society, but it is combined with an extraordinary patient and fatalistic endurance of hardship and pain.

Families are expected to support their members, and anyone from a large poor family who "makes good" is expected to support his or her relatives for many years. Because of this, eating in public is avoided unless the food is shared. In Ethiopian cities, rich and poor live in the same neighborhoods, and the incongruity of having slums nestling next to the opulent Sheraton and Hilton hotels elicits little comment from Ethiopians.

There has always been a wealthy class in Ethiopia, so poor people are used to discreet displays of wealth. Among the rich, wealth is not often flaunted, unless at a wedding. Among the large group of priests, monks, and generally devout people, wealth and luxury will be despised on ascetic grounds. However, there is now a growing desire for material things influenced from the West, and middle class people will now aspire to live in gated compounds to maintain their privacy.

Again, for ascetic or stoical reasons, pain is endured and sick people often do not consult a doctor unless the symptoms are very advanced. Both modern medicine and traditional medicine are used, simultaneously with holy water from a saint's shrine as an extra precaution.

ATTITUDES TO DEATH

When an Ethiopian dies, close mourners will beat their breasts and cry openly, while others maintain a respectful silence. The funeral follows very quickly, within twenty-four hours, as is the case in hot countries, and is always a burial, not a cremation (see page 76). The bodies of people who die overseas are often flown home for burial. During the burial procession Ethiopians, if driving past, will slow down and bow respectfully toward the deceased's coffin. Foreigners who drive past carelessly are considered very insensitive.

In the mourning tent erected near the deceased's home, callers will sit, normally in silence or quiet conversation. Wealthy Ethiopians will have a large memorial stone, or mausoleum, while Muslims will erect a more modest stone.

GENDER AND SEXUALITY

Women are not as subservient in Ethiopia as in some parts of the Middle East. In the early twentieth century Ethiopia had a female reigning empress, and a powerful Queen consort. Today, women are prominent in business, law, administration, and politics. Nevertheless, women are expected to cook and serve food for men, and commonly do this with easy grace.

In the countryside it is different. Women fetch water, and carry a large share of the tasks of rural life. Girls are sometimes married very young in the countryside, increasing the risks of death or injury in childbirth. The practice of female circumcision, more bluntly called female genital mutilation, remains widespread, but is not universal. The operation, designed to diminish sexual pleasure for women, is found among both Muslim and Christian peoples.

Although women are expected to be virgins until marriage, Ethiopian attitudes to sex are not puritanical. Heterosexual prostitution is not particularly shameful. However, gay sex is universally frowned upon. It is illegal for men, and assumed unthinkable for women. This does not mean that there is no homosexuality in Ethiopia, but it does mean that it is very much undercover, and seldom acknowledged. The Amharic for male gay sex is *Gebre Sodom*—sodomy.

The sexual abuse of young people by foreigners attracts severe penalties.

WORK ETHIC AND ATTITUDES TO TIME

Ethiopians are generally good at systematic, meticulous cerebral work. They have fine lawyers, accountants, airplane pilots, surgeons, and engineers. White-collar jobs, based at a desk, are more highly valued than those involving practical activity, trade, or manufacturing. People are often happier in a situation where they have carefully defined responsibilities, less content to be in a situation where there are no boundaries.

Written commitments are almost never broken. Verbal agreements are not as binding and for this reason are often preferred. Official letters from a company or an organization should always carry a seal, or ink stamps, as well as a signature.

People are wary about accepting checks, and cash continues to be the preferred method of payment. Cash payments should always be made against a receipt, and large sums should be paid in front of witnesses.

Ethiopians can generally be relied upon to be on time for appointments, although they refer self-deprecatingly to an *abasha ketero* ("Abyssinian appointment"), when they fear they may be late. It is recognized that it is not always easy to be on time in the face of Addis Ababa's sometimes horrendous traffic jams, and unpunctuality may be forgiven.

Foreign visitors are often surprised by a business phone call shortly after 7:00 a.m. Although normal working hours begin at 8:30 a.m., people are on the road early, and cell phones have made it easier to set up all the day's appointments before breakfast.

People do not generally phone each other after 9:30 p.m., and dinner parties should end at about that time.

In the countryside, timekeeping is not given such high value. People observe the cycles of the agricultural year and work when the need arises. They attend the weekly or twice weekly markets, sow and harvest their crops when the weather dictates, and take time off for the traditional communal activities such as attending church or celebrating a wedding.

In town or country, you will encounter a hardworking, early rising, meticulous, and methodical people.

chapter three

RELIGION & TRADITION

Very many Ethiopians are deeply religious; others at least respectful of religion. Orthodox Christian faith and practice is in a tradition unique to Ethiopia, more than half the population belonging to the Ethiopian Orthodox Church. About a third of Ethiopians are Muslim, mainly to the east and southeast of the country, and they follow the Sunni tradition of Islam. A significant minority belong to other Christian denominations, and there are animists, mostly among tribes to the south and west.

Ethiopia's tiny Jewish community has almost all emigrated, mostly to Israel, though immigrant West Indian Rastafarians, who follow the cult of Emperor Haile Selassie, are said to be increasing through immigration.

ORTHODOX CHRISTIANITY

Orthodoxy, as practiced in Ethiopia, is one of the closest to the early Christian Church. It is also strongly reliant on saintly intercessors, and has a canon that includes not only the books of the Bible, but also apocryphal books such as Enoch. It is not, however, a static Church, and the twentieth century affected it no less than Ethiopian life in general.

Saints of the Orthodox Church appear everywhere: in murals inside churches, in iconic representations sold on the street, and at sacred places associated with them. Mary, mother of Christ, is the most revered; Gebre Menfes Kiddus (known as *Abo*), associated with Mt. Zukwala, near Debre Zeit, is the "St. Francis" of Ethiopia, shown surrounded by animals; St. Tekle Haimanot is an historical figure from the thirteenth century, associated with Debre Libanos Monastery, shown standing on one leg (his other leg is shown alongside, because of the tradition that it became detached from his having stood for so many years in prayer). St. George, slayer of the dragon, conqueror of evil, is also popular. Of the archangels, Michael and Gabriel attract the largest number of devotees.

The Ethiopian Orthodox Church belongs to the Oriental Orthodox family of Christians, which also include the Egyptian Coptic, Armenian, Indian, and Syrian Churches. These Churches split from the rest of Christendom at the Council of Chalcedon in the fifth century. They are also known as monophysite, or *Tewahido*, because they describe Jesus Christ as "One incarnate nature of God the Word" (instead of "Two natures in One Person," a formula used by most other Christian Churches).

Christianity became the official religion of the Kingdom of Axum, northern Ethiopia, under King Ezana in about 330 CE. Tradition states that the faith was planted by two Christian brothers from Tyre, Frumentius and Edesius, who were shipwrecked on the coast. Frumentius was made the first bishop of the fledgling Church by Patriarch Athanasius in Egypt, and it was not until 1959 that the Ethiopian Orthodox Church became fully autonomous with the consecration of the first Ethiopian-born Patriarch, or *Abuna*. The Ethiopian Orthodox and Egyptian Coptic Churches, are in any case, very close in theology, liturgical style, and art.

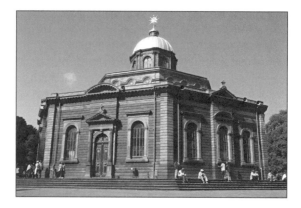

By the end of the fifth century there was a renewal in the Church influenced by Syrian refugees, now known as the "Nine Saints." In the sixth century one of their disciples, St. Yared, who "learnt his music from the birds," gave the Church its distinctive musical liturgy of chants, known as *zema*, in which the *debteras* (lay teachers and precentors) play an important role. Dressed in white garments they rattle the *sistra*, bang the drums, and dance as King David danced before the Holy of Holies. From about this time, too, churches were hewn from rocks and up cliff faces, many of them inhabited by hermits.

The Ethiopian Orthodox Church is also strongly marked by Jewish characteristics: Sabbath observance (although the main service is on a Sunday), the distinction between clean and unclean food, circumcision rites, and the idea of sexual uncleanness. Ethiopian Christians also have a deep respect for the St. Mary of Zion church in Axum, where the original Ark of the Covenant is said to be housed, after being spirited away for safekeeping when Solomon's temple was destroyed in Jerusalem. Only the guardian of this most holy of relics is allowed to set eyes on it. Every Ethiopian church has its replica of this Ark of the Covenant, known as a *tabot*. As in Jewish tradition, it is around the *tabot* that worship takes place, normally in the building, but outside when paraded on certain feast days.

The Church also shares a history of coexistence with Islam. Islamic tradition states that the prophet Mohammed, in the sixth century, advised his followers to take refuge in Ethiopia because he knew the Axumite king treated foreigners kindly. Muslims and Christians in Ethiopia are mostly tolerant of one another and their adherents make pilgrimage to each others' shrines, yet there is now a wariness that is exacerbated by events in other parts of the world.

Worship follows a weekly pattern of a Eucharist, in the form of a Liturgy (*Qidasse*), celebrated on Sundays. There is also a monthly cycle of saints' days, and an annual cycle of festivals that includes the main Church feasts of Fasika (Easter), Timket (Epiphany), and Meskel (Feast of the Exaltation of the Holy Cross). Services are led by several priests and many deacons, and often a choir with *debtera*. The priests alone are allowed behind an iconostasis inside the church, and they alone are allowed to handle the *tabot*.

The general public join in, or leave, at any point in the service, but only Orthodox are allowed communion. In practice only the very young or very old Ethiopians actually join the service inside the church and take communion, because of the view that between those ages they are sexually impure.

Most people are seen worshipping outside the doors of the church.

Visitors are welcome in Orthodox churches, provided they leave their shoes at the

door, cover their arms and legs, and respect
the Church's traditions.

The Orthodox Church today is no longer
tied to the State. It is now one of many Christian
denominations, a factor that has had an influence
on its internal dynamics and its sense of identity.
Translations of the Bible into the major Ethiopian
languages have led to a new renewal in the
Church. There is a central theological college,
and it takes its duty of caring for the poor
seriously, with an administrative branch at the
Synod office devoted to development projects.

MONASTIC LIFE

Monastic communities, both male and female,
exist alongside the formal Church. They follow
the pattern of the early Egyptian monasteries
founded by the fourth-century saints Anthony
and Pachomius. Many Ethiopian scholars were
nurtured in monasteries, and the monasteries
have been the preserve of literacy and
manuscripts down the centuries. Some
monasteries have had much influence in public
life. For example, Debra Libanos Monastery,
founded by St. Tekle Haimanot in the thirteenth
century. He it was who helped to restore the
Solomonic Emperors after the Zagwe dynasty
failed. The abbot, or leader, of a monastery is
known as *Memher* (meaning "teacher" in Ge'ez,
a title also applied to heads of large churches).
Differing schools of theology developed in
different monasteries, and these continue to
provide subjects for debate today.

As in other
Orthodox Churches
only unmarried
clergy are allowed
to become bishops;
these, and the
Patriarch (*Abuna*)
will be drawn from
the rank of monks.

Although no
longer influential
in public life,
monasteries continue to wield influence in the
private lives of Ethiopians. Pilgrimages are made
to monasteries for help with various troubles,
such as sickness or barrenness. Holy water may
be offered in bottles to take home as an efficacious
cure. The most popular today are Debra Libanos,
north of Addis Ababa; St. Mary
of Zion in Axum, the oldest church and guardian
of the Ark; the church of Egzabier Ab at Gishen
Monastery, having a fragment of the True Cross;
and St. Gabriel of Kulubi, near Dire Dawa.

Most popular of all, of course, for those who
can make it, is a pilgrimage to Jerusalem and a
visit to the piece of Ethiopia that is the roof of
the Church of the Holy Sepulchre—an area
unfortunately hotly contested with the Egyptian
Coptic Church. It is thought that the rock-hewn
churches at Lalibela, with their allusions to
Jerusalem, might have been built for those who
could not make the journey to the real Jerusalem.

Men and women can join monasteries at any
time of their lives. Many women will often join a

community of nuns when they become widowed and no longer have anyone to look after them. In both cases, they wear distinctive saffron yellow dress.

FASTING

Fasting is practiced by almost all Ethiopians, whether Christian or Muslim, and the requirements are kept according to the strictness with which the faith is practiced.

Orthodox Ethiopians from puberty onward will fast on Wednesdays and Fridays. Most will also keep the longer fasts during Lent (fifty-six days), Advent (forty days), and Kweskwam, the Feast of the Flight to Egypt (forty days). As many as 250 days of the year can be kept as fast days. Fasting implies having only one meal a day, usually after 3:00 p.m., and abstaining from meat and dairy products. Fish can be eaten during fasting, which is why it is not considered fit for a celebratory meal. Lentils and beans, especially *misr wot* (lentil stew) or *shiro wot* (chickpea stew) are the mainstays on fasting days.

Muslims fast during Ramadan, but this requires complete abstention from food or drink during the hours of daylight.

MAIN FEAST DAYS

In Ethiopia the Orthodox Church traditionally follows the Julian calendar, as do Orthodox Churches elsewhere, which runs thirteen days behind the Western, or Gregorian, calendar. As a result, Christmas and Epiphany in particular are celebrated later than in the West.

The most important Christian feast is Easter (Fasika), preceded by fifty-six days of fasting and daily services (Hudadi, or Abiy Tsom). Its date is moveable and is always on or after the Western date of Easter. Christmas (Liddet, or Genna) is preceded by a forty day fast and occurs on January 7 (Western calendar). All fasts are broken by great feasts in which quantities of meat are consumed. Cows and sheep are vigorously traded in the days up to this point, and mounds of bloodstained skins and fleeces at marketplaces mark the changeover to a carnivorous diet.

The most colorful celebrations are Epiphany (Timket) and the Feast of the Finding of the True Cross (Meskel) in late September. Timket celebrates the revelation of the divine Christ at his baptism in the Jordan River, whereas the Western Churches celebrate the revelation of Christ to the

nations through the three wise men. On the evening before Timket the whole church, with its congregation and the priests, carrying the *tabot*, processes to the nearest river to keep vigil. The next day, accompanied by enthusiastic drumming and chanting, the faithful dip in the river to renew their own baptismal vows, and the priests sprinkle holy water over the crowds.

Meskel is enjoyed because it marks the end of the *kremt* rains and anticipates the harvest. Ethiopians believe St. Helena was led to the cross by a fire, under which it was buried. Thus  bonfires are a big feature in this feast, and ashes are marked on the foreheads of worshippers, which are also spread on fields to ensure good crops.

BAPTISM

Baptism is one of the sacraments of the Church, along with confirmation, penance, Holy Communion, the Unction of the Sick, matrimony, and Holy Orders. It marks the "rebirth" of a child into the Christian family. Baptism takes place forty days after the birth of a boy, or eighty days for a girl. The rite is long and includes the churching of the mother and the purification of the child. The child is anointed thirty times with holy oil all over its body; it is then dipped three times in water while the Holy Trinity is invoked. Sponsors and godparents are appointed, as in Western Churches.

CATHOLIC CHRISTIANITY

Catholics are a significant minority of Christians. They have an archbishop based in Addis Ababa, and there are ten dioceses, including Adigrat in

Tigray, Addis Ababa and Endibir in SNNP region. They follow the Ethiopic liturgical rite, using Ge'ez, but they keep their own canon of biblical books and they are Chalcedonian in theology.

The presence of the Catholic Church in Ethiopia dates to the sixteenth-century Jesuit missions, which were caught up in politics as the Ethiopian emperors sought to fend off Muslim incursions. Later, Emperor Susenyos's conversion (c. 1607–32) to Catholicism became a brief, but significant, interlude in the reign of Orthodoxy. The Orthodox clergy were horrified by this apostasy. Susenyos was deposed after a civil war, and the Jesuit missionaries were evicted from the country. Catholic missions did not reappear until 1839, when, under St. Justin de Jacobis, the Church embraced the Ethiopic rite. Italians in Eritrea later influenced the spread of Catholicism in Ethiopia, as well as a number of influential missions in the south, particularly at Endibir.

PROTESTANT CHRISTIANITY

Protestant Christianity is growing very fast, especially in the west and south of the country.

Protestant missionaries appeared in Ethiopia in the mid-nineteenth century, who sought not to convert, but to act as agents for reform in the Ethiopian Orthodox Church. Some of these early missionaries were held captive by Emperor Tewodros and made to design and build large cannon for him. Such is the high regard in which Emperor Tewodros is now held in Ethiopia, that the largest of these cannon, nicknamed

Sebastopol, has a replica in Tewodros Square, on Churchill Avenue, Addis Ababa.

Other missionaries from Scandinavia and America arrived from the early twentieth century, and were given permission to operate mostly in the southern half of the country, where Ethiopian Orthodoxy had not gained much of a foothold. The fruit of this work is the growth of two particularly large Churches: the Kale Hewot, which derives from mostly American evangelical Christianity; and Mekane Yesus, which derives from mostly Scandinavian Lutheran Christianity. There are also a host of other Churches, many homegrown, and often charismatic in character.

Protestant theology, modern translations of the Bible into Amharic, and modern worship have sometimes influenced the Orthodox Church, and there are "reformed" Orthodox Churches in Addis Ababa, well-known for their Bible study and worship, especially among young people. However, change is not always well received in the Orthodox Church and some developments in the West, such as the ordination of women and homosexual priests, are seen as outright heresy by all the Churches.

ISLAM

Islam in Ethiopia is as old as the religion itself. The walled city of Harar is considered the fourth most holy city in Islam after Mecca, Medina, and Jerusalem, with 82 mosques and 102 shrines. The Prophet Mohammed advised those of his followers in Mecca who were being persecuted to go to northern Ethiopia, where they would "find a king who does not wrong anyone." These people later settled in Negash, Tigray, in 615 CE, now considered the home of Islam in East Africa. Both Muslims and Christians respect each other's shrines, the most important Islamic one being the twelfth-century Sheikh Hussein mosque to the east of the Bale Mountains.

However, relations were not always so sweet. In the sixteenth century a warlord, Mohammed Gragn, from the rising Emirate of Adal, nearly succeeded in overrunning the Christian kingdoms to the north, but was thwarted by a combined Ethio–Portuguese army. Later, the Ottoman Empire threatened Ethiopia's interests when it took the Red Sea coastal ports. The supposed conversion of Emperor Iyasu to Islam, in the early twentieth century, was one of the factors that led to his deposition. Today, relations on a personal level are mostly tolerant, though there are occasional reports of conflict in rural areas where one religion threatens the other. At a national level there is unease because of the threat from Islamic extremism in Somalia; and Saudi Arabian Wahabism, and its underwriting of mosques in town and country, is greeted with suspicion by all Christians.

CIRCUMCISION

Circumcision is widely practiced on both boys and girls. Circumcision for boys is, uniquely in Christian churches, practiced as a rite in Ethiopian Orthodoxy eight days after birth (another Jewish custom), and also among Muslims. Female circumcision is against the law in Ethiopia, but the law is not strongly enforced. Ethiopia has not yet ratified the African Union's Maputo Protocol (2005) against the practice.

TRADITIONAL BELIEFS

Apart from the three monotheistic religions, animistic beliefs and practices are to be found in Ethiopia, mainly in the south and west, and among the Oromo, and much syncretism of traditional beliefs with the main religions. Animism is practiced by tribal peoples, but there is also widespread practice of sorcery, divination, and astrology, particularly among rural people. Charms hung around the neck to ward off evil spirits, recourse to divining coffee dregs or fat from animals, are all encountered in places where life is most insecure and uncertain.

WEDDINGS

Marriages are made legal at a civil ceremony, but all ethnic groups and religions have their own customs to mark the occasion. Few Christians have a ceremony in church because of the strict conditions the Church sets for marriage: divorce is not allowed by those married in church, for example, and Ethiopians traditionally have had a liberal view of divorce and remarriage. Marriages are usually negotiated between the two families by a mediator, a role also used by diaspora Ethiopians who seek a wife from home.

When a wedding takes place, it is a protracted affair that can take several days, during which there is a boisterous and noisy cavalcade of hooting cars (see also pages 96 and 105). Pride of place goes to the cameraman perched in a car that drives back and forth to catch every moment. Woe betide those who get in the way. Westerners can be invited to any part of the wedding, though it is likely to be the main meal, when smart clothes should be worn.

The giving of presents by guests is not as common in Ethiopia as in the West. The pinning of money to the bridal couple for luck during dancing at the reception is done, but not at very posh weddings. The bridegroom presents the bride with a trousseau of dresses to which she is supposed to express scorn, but to accept them nevertheless.

In the Oromo countryside you might come across a wedding celebration. You'll see a party of traditional horsemen, their steeds ornately and colorfully saddled and bridled, galloping about in good-natured drunkenness.

FUNERALS

A white tent pitched in the street alongside a house is a sure sign of a funeral. These are very important events that involve the whole community. The family will probably be a member of an *idir,* a self-help funeral insurance club, which mobilizes to make decisions and pay the funeral costs.

When a person dies, mourners gather at the deceased's home to comfort the family and make arrangements. The tent (*denkwan*) is ordered to provide seating space, the women will generally prepare food for the mourners, and the men will make other practical arrangements such as ordering the coffin. The burial takes place within a day or two of death, in a graveyard near the church, and is conducted by a priest, if Christian. The *denkwan* will remain for several more days to enable all the mourners to pay their respects. It is usual to make a point of greeting the most closely bereaved, then to sit quietly and somberly in chairs placed around the *denkwan* for a suitable length of time, and then quietly take your leave after you have been offered something to eat.

It is worth noting that the *idir* is a very important social grouping in its own right. They gather members together regularly to make decisions about funds, and the funds themselves might also be used for times of hardship, or credit.

All Ethiopians, not just Christians, are buried quickly after death. Wealthy Christians mark their graves with large headstones or mausoleums. Oromo are buried in colorful graves in the countryside, often decorated with birds and animals. The Konso in the south are animists and their wooden funeral statues are well-known. Muslims are buried in their own graveyards. There is a foreign cemetery with sections for Armenians, Greeks, and other Europeans— including those who died during the fighting to liberate Ethiopia in 1940–41—in Gulele on the western outskirts of Addis Ababa.

COFFEE CEREMONY AND STIMULANTS
The taking of coffee at an Ethiopian home is an unhurried, elaborate ritual. Although the custom

of drinking hot, roasted coffee is thought to have been invented in Arabia, such is the pride Ethiopians have for Arabica coffee—which has its origins in the country and is now its biggest export—that legends have grown around it.

Every woman, and many men, is practiced at roasting coffee. On special occasions rushes are spread about the floor and decorated with flowers.

The washed green beans are roasted dry in a pan over a hot brazier. When the beans crackle, the smoke is wafted toward the guests to whet their senses, and incense is burnt to mingle with the smoke. When ready, the roasted beans are taken away and pounded in a mortar. Meanwhile, water is put to boil in a clay coffeepot (*jebena*) after which the coffee is brewed in it. The coffee is then carefully poured into twelve small cups, representing the apostles. Sugar, and occasionally salt, are added to taste. Visitors should try to accept three pourings: the first is known as *abol* in Amharic, the second *huletegna*, and the third is the blessing, known as *bereka*. Roasted peanuts or barley (*kollo*) are handed around to accompany the coffee.

Much older is the custom of mashing coffee leaves or roasted beans, and mixing the grounds with butter. This is then used as a stimulant by travelers, or by monks needing to pray all night.

Chat (also transliterated as *khat*, or *qat*, especially in Arabic), a stimulant containing amphetamine, is widely grown and used. It is also one of the highest value exports. It is normally chewed as part of a social ritual among Muslims in Yemen and Somalia, as well as in Ethiopia. It grows where coffee grows, attracts a higher price than coffee, and it is now chewed more widely, particularly by the younger generation, to help them through exams or hardship. For this reason there is considerable disapproval of it. *Chat* is illegal in the USA, Canada, and many parts of Europe.

TIME AND CALENDAR

Ethiopia traditionally follows the Coptic calendar still in use in Egypt, and uses an era that is seven years and eight months behind the Western Gregorian calendar. On September 12, 2007, Ethiopia celebrated its new millennium.

The extra five days tagged onto the twelve thirty-day months of the Coptic calendar is reckoned as a "thirteenth month." Government documents all use the Coptic calendar, so care should be taken when using such documents.

The time of day is also reckoned differently. This follows the traditional Middle Eastern twelve-hour clock, when the hours are counted from dawn, being 6:00 a.m. Thus 9:00 a.m. is three o'clock in Ethiopia, and twelve noon is six o'clock.

Aware of these differences, Ethiopians will usually remember when talking with foreigners to be precise about which calendar or timing they are using. Reference to the Western, or European, calendar is made; and to Ethiopian or European time when the clock is mentioned.

chapter four

MAKING FRIENDS

Ethiopians value long-term friendships. These often go back to childhood and school days, and extend beyond family, tribe, and religious background. An Ethiopian friendship requires and exhibits deep loyalty, and may well involve the sharing of all kinds of material resources, such as cars and houses, as well as the less demanding expectations of attendance at weddings, funerals, and other family events. In the event of grave sickness or other serious family trouble, an established friendship will require one to drop everything, and make oneself available to help in whatever way is needed.

ETHIOPIANS AND FOREIGNERS
Making friends is apparently easy at a superficial level, but deeper relationships will require interaction over a number of years. Friendships between Ethiopians and foreigners are frequent, and longstanding foreign residents can expect to

find themselves wholly integrated into the community. However Ethiopians and foreigners who become friends occasionally do experience disappointment if expectations of what is to be gained from that friendship differ.

Ethiopians have a long established culture of care of guests. This can involve simple kindnesses, like an invitation to a foreigner to share, or the offer to pay for, a cup of coffee, a glass of beer, or a soft drink. They may be disappointed if this approach is not reciprocated. On the other hand only people with an ulterior motive will offer too much too soon. Be wary of anyone who seems to be too pressing in their attempts to build a friendship; they may be trying to box you into position where you cannot say no to a request for an expensive favor.

When entering into relationships with foreigners, Ethiopians are also often a little wary. It is as well to remember that Ethiopians may regard foreigners as technically and sometimes materially superior, but they will also regard Western culture as morally inferior to their own, particularly in its inadequate sense of family loyalty, and its attitude to old people. Since some Westerners come to Ethiopia in order to "do good" among people who are poor, and some come with their own, unacknowledged, sense of moral superiority, a clash can occur in the interaction between Ethiopian and Westerner.

INVITATIONS HOME

If you receive an invitation to an Ethiopian home for a meal, you can safely take a cake or flowers as a present. In return, expect an Ethiopian to present you with a cake bought from a patisserie when visiting your home.

Ethiopians, whoever they are, are not shy of inviting foreigners to their homes, and evenings and weekends after work are usually the chosen times. In more traditional homes, wives will do the cooking, but not take part in the meal, with any children or servants helping. At the very least, coffee is usually offered and, depending on the level of the invitation, this is done as a ceremony with the coffee being roasted on a brazier in front of the guests, and grass and flowers placed on the floor in their honor. The conversation at such times can often follow intellectual discussions on such topics as religion, philosophy, and politics, and the fortunes of Manchester United and Arsenal football (soccer) clubs. If food is offered, it will be traditional Ethiopian, with *injera* (a type of pancake), and various *wots* (stews). Western bread, and non-spicy foods, may also be offered, specially prepared for a foreign guest, but appreciation of Ethiopian food will be welcomed.

It is good manners, in dealing with *injera* and *wot* meals, to use only the right hand to eat with,

as the left is considered unclean. It is also common practice to leave a small piece of *injera* uneaten on your plate, when you have finished, to show that you have had your fill. If you do not do this, you may be pressed to eat more than you want. It is also sometimes the custom for an Ethiopian host to feed his guests by hand, preparing a small roll of *injera* with *wot*, and putting it directly in the guest's mouth. If this is unwelcome, it is enough to explain that it is not your custom, to avoid giving offense.

HOW DO YOU MEET ETHIOPIANS?

Ethiopians are ready enough to talk to complete strangers, but genuine friendships most often begin with an introduction, or with a common professional or business interest. Foreigners and Ethiopians work together in a variety of contexts—academic, medical, technical, and diplomatic.

It is also possible to meet ordinary people in bars, hotels, and restaurants, but you will need to be aware of the status of the place you are meeting in. Addis Ababa has a huge variety of restaurants, bars, and nightclubs. Expectations of what you will encounter in them can be confusing to the newcomer.

MEN AND WOMEN—CROSS-CULTURAL RELATIONSHIPS

Intermarriage between Ethiopians and foreigners is not at all unusual, especially between Ethiopian women and men from the Eastern Mediterranean, who have been settling in the country for centuries. Romance and marriage between Ethiopians and Western foreigners is also becoming increasingly common. These relationships are often very happy and successful, though of course they can and do incur cross-cultural strains. For example, Western women can find that their husband's relatives from the countryside outstay their welcome, and they also come in very large numbers. They will also find that the terms "aunt," "uncle," "sister," and "brother" are expanded to include many other extended family members, as well as those adopted into the family. The same courtesy should be given to them as to close family members. On the other hand, an Ethiopian woman can find her foreign husband's unwillingness to support older members of the family—for instance by inviting his mother-in-law to join them in their home in the West— very galling indeed.

There are also a number of marriages between older Western men and much younger Ethiopian women. The Ethiopian wife in this case may have ambitions to find economic security, and be affronted if this is not on offer. In parallel with this are the cases of very young Ethiopian men who marry older foreign women, and become rapidly disillusioned if a visa and move to the West do not materialize quite soon after the wedding.

In contemplating these things, the visitor to Ethiopia needs to be aware that marriage here, even in the more traditional parts of the country, is not always a lifelong relationship. Exploitative relationships between men and women are no more unknown in Ethiopian culture than they are in the West. Divorce, and extramarital relationships, are as common in the countryside as they are in the cities. Gay sexual relationships are frowned upon, and are illegal between men;

any visitor to Ethiopia who is so inclined should be aware of this.

LOW LIFE

All Ethiopian towns have bars, euphemistically translated in Amharic as *buna bet*, or "coffeehouse." Respectable women are almost never to be seen in these bars, some of which double up as brothels or hotels. There will be plenty of alcohol on sale, and perhaps not much coffee. A male traveler who gets sexually involved with a prostitute does so at his peril. HIV/AIDS is very common.

It is just possible that a visitor may be invited to a *chat* chewing session. The Muslim tradition of chewing *chat* is spreading throughout the whole Ethiopian community. *Chat* is a shrub, from which fresh clippings are taken daily. When chewed, it acts as mild narcotic from the amphetamines in it, bringing energy and elation to begin with, somnolence and confusion later. Chewing *chat* is a common but not, except perhaps in Harar culture, a respectable activity. A visitor can say no to this with dignity, and little offense will be taken.

AVOIDING EXPLOITATION IN RELATIONSHIPS

Relationships between equals often work the best. This rules out exploitation by inducing feelings of guilt about material inequality, and is generally attainable between Ethiopians and foreigners who know each other well, whatever their material, educational, or social status.

There are however some relationships that become exploitative. Ethiopians and foreigners have different ways of exploiting each other. Some foreigners, who make friends in order to find a business partner, to find romance, or to get around the country, mistake the loyalty of Ethiopians in friendship and forget to offer reciprocal courtesies, or that Ethiopians also need to balance the demands of their homes and families with time spent with their foreign friends.

There are some foreigners, particularly Middle Easterners, but also others, who employ Ethiopian girls as domestics for very low wages, and expect a high level of service over very long hours. There is little personal relationship on offer. In Ethiopia domestic servants will expect to be treated on human terms, and may well invite you to their homes. You should reciprocate at least by getting to know employees personally, and by offering fair wages and fair treatment. They will appreciate a gift on your return from abroad, and a tip from any guests who are staying with you.

Ethiopians often exploit Westerners by various forms of begging. This can range from begging in the street or in traffic queues, to requests for money delivered by letter or at a prearranged private interview. You may find yourself having to deal with the flattering suggestion that only you can understand, because of your especially compassionate nature, the particular difficulties of the person making the request. It is a mistake to fall for this kind of flattery. You can safely say "No."

GREETINGS AND FAREWELLS

Ethiopians greet their friends and family, including their foreign friends, in various ways, often with an embrace and a kiss on each cheek, and again on the first side, if they have not seen each other for a long time, but always at least by shaking hands. It is conventional for each party to ask the other if they are well, and to reply that they are (even if they are not!), and to add *"Egziabher Yimesgen,"* which means "Thanks be to God." Muslims often prefer to say *"Alhamdulillah,"* which means the same thing in Arabic.

When you arrive back in the country after a long period away, your Ethiopian friends will all come around to your house to greet you, or invite you to their homes for a meal. When returning overseas, friends may insist on giving you a present, often a souvenir of Ethiopia, to take home with you—it might be T-shirts for your children, or a bag of coffee beans for you to roast in your own country.

Saying good-bye generally involves a form of words meaning "be well"—in Amharic, *Dehna hunu*. If you have been visiting Ethiopians at home, they will generally come to the door, to your car, or the gate of their compound to see you out. Doing this is called *meshenyet*, or "accompanying," in Amharic. If you are leaving Ethiopia for good after a long stay, you may find a large meal has been prepared for you as a farewell and people will come with you to the airport to see you off as they would their own families.

THE ETHIOPIANS AT HOME

THE HOME AND THE COMPOUND

Ethiopians favor the traditional compound (or enclosure) as a model for their home life. It provides security and room for their extended family to share a common life.

In the Ethiopian countryside a family will live in a thatched house built of mud and wood, or stone, and almost always surrounded by a wall, or a fence with a gateway. There may be two or three houses within the enclosure, belonging to members of an extended family. The enclosure is

known as a *gebi* in Amharic, and this is always translated in English as "compound." This pattern has been adapted to fit the urban lifestyle of Addis Ababa and other large towns, where middle-class people build themselves a family home, surrounded by a wall

or a fence, with a big front gate. This constitutes
a compound. Current planning regulations in
Addis Ababa, where land is scarce, favor a
multistory building, with a very small compound,
but houses that go back twenty-five years or more
are likely to be one-story villas with a rather larger
garden space.

Poorer people in the cities will rent one or two
rooms in a compound owned by a private
landlord, or by the *kebele,* roughly equivalent to
a community council, the lowest unit of local
government in both city and countryside. This
kind of accommodation is rapidly being replaced
by condominiums, blocks of apartments built to
a standard design, and not more than four stories
high. Urban society is still adjusting to the
changes in lifestyle these apartments entail.

THE FAMILY

The family unit in Ethiopia extends to brothers
and sisters and their children, sons and daughters
who have not been able to establish themselves in
their own home, and their spouses and children.
Elderly parents may also be accommodated in the
family home. Middle-class families are also likely
to have some live-in servants, and there may be a
separate series of rooms at the back of the
compound for them.

Most modern homes will have a living room
with a few armchairs, or a sofa surrounding a low
table, and if there is room, a dining table with
upright chairs. Almost everybody aspires to own a
television, and this will be prominent in the living

room. The traditional dining table in Ethiopia is a *mesob,* a three-foot-high basket with a shallow rim, fitted to a basket ware base, in which a tray containing *injera* and *wot* can be placed. Even if this is not regularly used in a modern household, it is likely that there will be one somewhere on display in the living room. In the kitchen, or in a cabinet with cups on display, will be all the equipment needed for making food, including the means for roasting and brewing coffee in the traditional manner. In a modern home the cooking facility is likely to be electricity or propane gas, or there will be a small brazier using charcoal, or a Chinese-made kerosene stove, which can be placed on the floor.

Eating together is an important part of Ethiopian life. Given that people, in town and country, need to rise early and leave for work early, they will often take a light breakfast, have their lunch either at an eating house, or out of a lunch box, and then have a family meal at about 7:00 p.m. Most people will expect to be in bed by 9:30 p.m.

The family home will also be decorated with religious pictures, or biblical texts, and family photographs. There may also be artificial or real flowers around the house, particularly in the Ethiopian spring after the rains in September.

LIFE'S ROUTINES

Orthodox Christians are regular churchgoers. Many will have a close link to a church dedicated to a particular saint or archangel, and they will attend that church early on Sunday mornings, and on regular church festivals.

If they belong to a *mehaber,* a church-based association, each member will provide hospitality for the other members, and receive hospitality from them in turn, on a regular basis. A *mehaber* can also function as a savings club, called *ikub,* and as a funeral society, so that the cost of a funeral, and the hospitality costs associated with it, does not fall on a single family at a time of bereavement. The *ikub* members all contribute a fixed sum every month to a central kitty, and then each takes the whole kitty when it is their turn to do so. This works as a form of life assurance, or micro-finance bank.

Catholic and Protestant Christians will also devote their Sundays to Church activities. Protestants, however, do not observe saints' days, and do not generally observe the fasting regulations of the Church.

Muslims will generally attend Friday midday prayers at the mosque, and will also observe Ramadan. As Sunday remains the official day of rest, they may go out to lunch at a restaurant, or on a picnic that day. Picnics, if taken, are generally at a park outside town, or in an enclosure just on the edge of a main road, enhanced with flower beds and chairs and tables.

In the countryside, attendance at markets, which happen weekly, or sometimes twice weekly in small towns, is a social as well as a commercial activity. Many of these towns take their names from their market day—for example, "Thursday Market"—and the townspeople provide services

for those who come to it. Sellers and buyers may often have to walk many miles to reach the market, and if they do well on a sale, they will often refresh themselves for the walk home with a glass or two of *tella*, a drink made from barley that is similar to beer, or *tej*, a stronger alcoholic drink made from fermented honey.

In Addis Ababa markets are important too. The main market of Addis Ababa, called the Mercato, is said to be Africa's largest market, and is home to one of the city's most important business communities. There are also smaller markets in various parts of the city with covered stalls selling most of what might be needed in the kitchen. At various points are places where sheep and goats are also traded. These smaller markets are located on the periphery of the city center.

DAILY WORK

Most middle-class Ethiopian families can only get by if both husband and wife are working. This means that everybody gets up early, the children are packed off to school, and the adults are in a taxi or a bus by about 7:30 am.

If the family is wealthy enough, or is joined by a young relative from the countryside, there will be a servant or two to manage the household, usually female. This person is responsible for preparing breakfast, sweeping floors, washing clothes (by hand), and buying ingredients from the local market, kiosk, or small supermarket. Meat is bought fresh from a butcher who has slaughtered it according to the required Christian or Muslim ritual, or on the hoof. Chickens are usually bought live, then killed and plucked at home.

Evenings may be spent helping children with their homework or watching television. On weekends there is time for sports or a visit to a park.

In the countryside, much depends on the agricultural season, whether it is plowing, planting, or harvesting time. No one is idle for long for everything is done by hand, from taking stones out of a pile of pulses, to sorting the seeds from last year's harvest into categories that maximize their growing potential for the next. Rivers are great social centers, for that is where women go as a group to wash their clothes, or to collect water; there, they meet their friends, pass gossip, and reinforce bonds. If a woman finds her domestic work for the day is finished she will then likely be making handicrafts such as weaving a colored basket. Boys, often as young as five years, are usually given the responsible task of looking after the family's animals while they graze outside the compound. At night they are brought into the compound to protect them from theft or wild animals.

GROWING UP IN ETHIOPIA

In town or country, every family will hope to send their children to school, hopefully for the complete twelve-year syllabus, but certainly for the eight years of primary and junior secondary. There was a time when girls would drop out of school earlier than boys because of either early marriage, or the need for them to help domestically, but in much of Ethiopia this is no longer the case.

The state provides free education, and both in the countryside and in Addis Ababa capacity constraints have led to a shift system, in which each classroom is used for two shifts by day, and for evening classes as well. Children will walk up to nine miles (fifteen kilometers) a day to attend school. Private education is developing fast, and many families in the major cities will go to great lengths to pay for this in order to get a longer school day, and for the possibility of learning

English. Private schools run a regular school day
from about 9:00 a.m. to about 3:30 p.m. Middle-
class parents generally hire a taxi or a shared
minibus to take their children to school.

Recent years have seen a huge expansion in the
provision of both state and private higher
education. Many Ethiopian families also now
wish to provide this opportunity for their
children, which means that offspring of college-
age often continue to live at home, or with
relatives in the larger towns, until well into their
twenties. Wealthier families often look for a
university education abroad for their children,
in India, in Europe, or in North America.
Universities in Ethiopia, both private and state
funded, are expanding every year.

Service in the army, which is no longer
compulsory, provides opportunities for young
people from the countryside to get away from
home, and join the wider Ethiopian society.

MARRIAGE

There are two quite different patterns for marriage in Ethiopia, the ancient and the modern.

In modern Addis Ababa, and in the bigger cities, people get married at almost any age between twenty and fifty. Men in particular will leave the decision to get married until they are economically established, and this may take a long time. Many urban women find it quite hard to find a partner, and some remain unmarried for life. Young people will expect to choose their own partner, and they will not expect their families to interfere with their choice. When they do get married, they may convert from the Christian faith to Islam, or vice versa; this is now quite acceptable among educated people.

In the countryside the traditional pattern persists. Young men expect to marry and set up a home at eighteen or younger, their brides often as young as thirteen or fourteen. Although there is official discouragement of this practice from both secular and religious authorities, it still persists despite the dangers, for example, of childbirth before the girl has fully grown up. Arranged marriages do occur, particularly for daughters in their very early teens, often to much older men, and largely for economic reasons—sometimes girls run away from home to the cities to avoid such marriages.

As we have seen, marriage ceremonies, whether in town or countryside, have certain common elements. In the city there will be processions of cars and limousines, decorated with ribbons and flowers, to collect the bride from her home, bring her to the ceremony, to take the newly married couple for photographs in a park, and then on to a reception where there will be tables groaning with food, including raw meat, supplied in the form of a carcass, from which a butcher will chop a helping for each guest.

In the countryside there will be brightly caparisoned horses, instead of vehicles, and a blowing of brass trumpets instead of car horns. The reception will be held in a tent rather than a hotel, but the basic pattern of the ceremony will be the same.

A priest may be on hand to add a blessing, but only committed Orthodox Christians will be married in church: divorce is not permitted for those who have married in church. In that case the religious ceremony will take place during the early morning liturgy on a Saturday or Sunday, and all the rest of the proceedings will follow.

DEATH AND MOURNING

A funeral is always a significant occasion, and the whole community will attend. In the countryside this means a whole village or small town joining in. In cities it means friends and family, and work colleagues, of the deceased. There are no cremations. Orthodox and Protestant Christians, and Muslims, are buried in separate cemeteries.

After the burial, the mourning tent will be put up, in which food and drink will be served to the mourners. For several days afterward bereaved members of the family will sit in it and receive the condolences of friends and relatives. Most will come and sit in silence, or converse in low voices for between thirty and sixty minutes. If a foreigner or a visitor has had any kind of relationship with the person who has died, then they should at least attend and sit in the tent for a brief time. Flowers should not be brought or sent to a funeral in Ethiopia.

People will wear black for up to a year following the death of a close relative.

THE YEAR'S ROUND

As we have seen, Ethiopia follows a calendar of Coptic, or Egyptian, origin and the routine follows both religious and agricultural cycles.

The major festivals are public holidays, and are occasions for people to visit their hometown for a few days, or to stay at home with family. These include: New Year, on September 11; Meskel, on September 29, which coincides with the end of the *kremt*, the season of the big rains; Christmas, on January 7; and Epiphany, on January 19. Easter and the major Muslim festivals have moveable dates. Besides attending the church services and religious ceremonies that these festivals imply, people will celebrate by breaking their fast, whether of Lent or Ramadan, and eating meat. Families will buy a chicken or a sheep, or take a share in an ox, and these animals will be slaughtered early in the morning of the day of the festival.

People will also sometimes visit a vacation resort for a festival. The nearest thing that Ethiopia has to a beach resort is the shore of Lake Langano, in the Rift Valley. Now crowded with hotels, this offers a place to swim or lie in the sun. Other favorite resorts for Addis Ababa residents are Sodere, near Adama (or Nazareth), and Awassa in the Rift Valley.

Apart from festivals, Ethiopians seem to take few vacations, often accumulating several months of annual leave over several years, and then perhaps taking three months off to visit a relative or friend in America or Europe.

In the countryside, the rhythms of agriculture are more significant. The fields are plowed before the big rains (*kremt*) in May, and sown with grain crops in June or July, so that they will ripen after the rains end in September. They will then be harvested, threshed, and winnowed by December. Other crops—such as lentils, chickpeas, and beans— follow their own cycle, but all will be complete by

Christmas, or soon after. During the long, dry, hot months that follow, nothing much can be sown unless there are satisfactory short rains in March or April, or unless an adjacent river provides irrigation possibilities. In this situation people grow crops of pumpkin, onions, or tomatoes.

The question asked every year is whether there will be short rains, and whether they will be sufficient for a harvest before the big rains in July.

In the south and west, coffee prices and annual yields are crucial to millions of people. Some years produce a bumper crop, other years do not. World prices go up and down and, with modern communications, even the remotest growers are aware of what their product is worth from day to day. The beginning of the new coffee harvest each year after the rains is important to all.

DRESS

A throng of people at a market or outside a church will mostly be wearing white: shawls, head scarves, dresses, and men's jodhpurs, mostly made from locally woven cotton. Only in Muslim and lowland areas such as Harar is there more color.

Although Western dress is the norm in the cities, and is replacing traditional rural dress, on special occasions most Ethiopians revert to the traditional style, sometimes updated. Women wear a basic long white cotton kaftan, drawn at the waist by a colored tie, and an embroidered inset around the bottom. Depending on wealth or status, the embroidery is wider and more ornate.

Every Ethiopian woman will have a selection of dresses, often provided as a trousseau on marriage.

A man's smart dress is also white: a pair of white jodhpurs, or loose trousers, with a short white kaftan on top, and the outfit finished with white shoes. The only colors to creep into this all-white attire are likely to be those of the Ethiopian flag—red, green, and yellow—which may be sewn into a seam or around the brim of a hat.

A shawl thrown around the shoulders or over the head, also of white cotton, known as a *shama* ("woven"), is worn mostly by women. The thicker *gabi* is essential in the cooler highlands.

In the city, although Western fashion prevails, the school uniform for young girls is generally a modest ankle-length skirt. Muslim women will invariably wear a longer skirt and a head scarf.

DRINKING COFFEE

Coffee is Ethiopia's national beverage. People believe that it takes its Western name from the province of Kafa in southwest Ethiopia, and that it was "discovered" for the world by an Ethiopian goatherd named Kaldi. Coffee in Amharic is *buna,* and, as we have seen, the drinking of it is accompanied by much custom and ceremony. It is drunk throughout Ethiopia, and village women will invite each other to drink it just as eagerly as middle-class women in Addis Ababa. It is always served after a meal with guests.

chapter six

TIME OUT

Leisure activities in Ethiopia vary from traditional games, to modern sports, to intellectual sparring over a glass of whiskey. Many a coffeehouse is the scene of the kindling of friendships, restaurants host evening trysts, and parks are popular for walks with family and friends. Urban Ethiopians find time after work or on weekends for these things, whereas rural people, tied to the land, are more likely to combine traditional pursuits with religious and national days. Family or community obligations, such as weddings and funerals, are *de rigueur*. Particularly religious individuals will make time for devotions to their favorite saint or go on pilgrimage.

Ethiopians are not at all shy of inviting foreigners to join them at home, especially for family events and on religious days. In turn, they, with their sense of curiosity, will gladly accept a foreigner's invitation to a meal at their home, a concert, or a foray to a tourist site out of town. However, since urban Ethiopians on the whole prefer bright lights to the silence of the countryside, they might prefer a visit to a spa or town outside Addis Ababa to hiking up a bare mountainside. It is always worth asking, however, as there will be exceptions to this generalization.

PUBLIC HOLIDAYS

Ethiopians enjoy thirteen public holidays, celebrating Christian or Islamic holy days and important national events.

September 11: New Year's Day in the Ethiopian calendar (St. John's Day). Marked by bonfires and a holiday

September 27: Feast of Meskel, which celebrates the finding of the true cross in Jerusalem by St. Helena, and the end of the rains

January 7: Christmas (Genna), preceded by fasting

January 19: Epiphany, or the Baptism of Christ (Timket). An especially colorful ceremony when priests parade the churches' *tabots* around a pool or stream, and sprinkle the crowd with holy water

March 2: Victory at Adwa Day. A secular holiday celebrating Menelik II's victory over the Italians in 1896

March to April: Good Friday and Easter Day, moveable feasts, usually later than their Western equivalents, and the most important Christian days, preceded by a long fast

May 1: International Labor Day

May 5: Ethiopian Patriots' Victory Day, which marks the downfall of the Italian Fascist occupation in 1941

May 28: Downfall of the Derg Regime in 1991

The Muslim festivals of Id Al Fater (marking the end of Ramadan), Id Al Adaha (Feast of Sacrifice), and Maulid, (which celebrates the Prophet Mohammed's birthday), follow dates in the Islamic lunar calendar and are celebrated a few weeks earlier every year.

Although individuals largely dislike being photographed in an ordinary context, they do not mind if you are taking photographs of them at a major festival.

AFTER WORK AND WEEKENDS

For Ethiopians in employment weekends and evenings are a time for regrouping and relaxing. It will be a time to be with their school-age children or, if unmarried, a time to be with friends, and go to a café or a bar. Many people who are trying to

better themselves with extra qualifications will often take the opportunity to put in extra study, or go to night school.

Traditional games like *Gabeta* (a board game played with stones and a number of holes), and Ethiopian chess, were once played regularly in the home. Today, they have given way to television,

which will often be on in the corner of a room as
much for its background sound as for actual
viewing. Television screens are also in view in
bars, hotels, and other public places—useful for
those who cannot afford a television at home.
Satellite television, featuring CNN and
international sports channels, is often available
in the most remote locations. The fortunes of top
English and Italian football teams are followed
throughout the land.

WEDDINGS AND FAMILY EVENTS

Weddings, we have seen, are major social events.
There will normally be a ceremony of some sort
in church or a hotel, followed by a drive about the
city in convoy, all captured on video. This will be
followed by the reception, with tables laden with
food, including raw meat. There will also be a
band and normally a soloist singing traditional
songs. A few days later there will be a second
reception (*mels*), traditionally hosted by the
bride's family.

If you are invited to a wedding feast, do dress
smartly. You do not need to take a present.
Banknotes may be pinned to the clothes of the
bride and groom at rural weddings.

Ethiopians only reluctantly leave their children
behind when they attend a social occasion, and
young children can be seen late into the night in
restaurants. Middle-class Ethiopians will also
lavish attention and money on children's
birthday parties.

MENAFESHA

Ethiopians like taking the air. There are many recreation parks, known as *Menafesha*—literally, a place for getting fresh air—generally on the

outskirts of a town or city, where people go to relax, enjoy beer or fizzy drinks, and sometimes piped music. There will be trees and flowering shrubs, and tables and chairs under a gazebo or awning of some sort; and they will vary from the very posh, to a simple affair for those with less cash to spare. Weddings and other parties can be held at a *Menafesha*, or they may call in at one between the ceremony and the meal, for photographs among the flowers. Some *Menafesha* have merry-go-rounds and swings for children.

SPAS

Ethiopians love their hot water spas. Addis Ababa was built near a spa, called by the Oromo name, Finfinne (*Filwoha* in Amharic), which the Empress Taitu patronized at the end of the nineteenth century. This now supplies hot water for public baths, graded and priced accordingly, where a bath followed by a traditional Ethiopian meal can be had. Swimming pools at both the Hilton and Ghion hotels in Addis Ababa are heated by hot springs.

Outside Addis Ababa, the resorts popular with Ethiopians are at Sodere, near Adama, with its two heated swimming pools, and at Ambo, two hours drive west of Addis Ababa, and the home of Ethiopia's most popular bottled mineral water. Middle-class Ethiopians might go for a weekend with their children, or a group of unmarried Ethiopians. For those who do not have a car, it is often the choice for a bus outing.

ETHIOPIAN CUISINE AND DRINK

Cooking is a high art with a huge variety of dishes normally seen at their best at a wedding or special occasion. Most dishes are infused with *berbere*, a spice mixture containing very hot chili pepper. At home Ethiopians traditionally eat communally from one platter; they eat in a reserved way—it is considered impolite to stuff oneself—and, instead of cutlery, they use their right hand, which if used clumsily, should never be licked.

The staple grain is *teff*, which is made up into a giant pancake (*injera*) that covers a two-foot diameter plate. On this various tasty stews (*wot*) and other dishes are piled. Guests sit around and help themselves to *injera*, which they wrap around any stews of their choice. At a less formal meal, the *injera* is cut up and served in rolls on a central platter, with each person taking a roll and helping themselves to the sauces, vegetables, and *wot* of their choice.

The *wot* is a cooked stew made out of meat, including chicken (*doro wot*), mutton (*ye beg wot*), and beef (*ye bere sega*). A commonly found dish is fried meat known as *tibs* (literally, "fried"). A stew without peppers is known as *alicha*—Ethiopians are usually conscious of the fact that many Westerners cannot take the heat of Ethiopian dishes, and so provide at least one or two of this type. *Kitfo* is very lightly cooked, or raw minced meat. Cottage cheese (*ayb*) and various vegetables, including

Ethiopia's own cabbage (*goman*), are added. Puddings as such are rare, fresh fruit being handed around after a meal, but cakes are much appreciated, especially in coffeehouses.

On fasting days *misr wat* (lentils), *shiro wat*, made from ground chickpeas, and fish are allowed.

Honey is highly prized in Ethiopia, given to children as a sweet drink called *berz*, or an alcoholic beverage known as *tej* for adults. *Talla* is the local beer, which is made from barley and flavored with a herb called *geisho*.

In Sidamo and Gurage the staple is a food made from *enset* (false banana); maize is grown and used in southern areas; and sorghum is used for making *injera* in those areas where *teff* cannot be grown. In the east, Somali foods, such as goat meat and rice, are more common.

EATING OUT AND BARS

Ethiopians love to eat out, and go to nightclubs and bars if young and unmarried. They prefer their traditional food, but there are many foreign dishes that, when spiced up, have been adapted to the Ethiopian taste. For example, the Ethiopian version of spaghetti bolognese consists of a tomato sauce richly endowed with chili peppers or *berbere*.

Most towns have a modern hotel where the more affluent Ethiopians might be found dining out; simple meals, such as an omelette (again spiced with chili peppers), are generally available in roadside restaurants. Since Ethiopians do not like to eat in public, chairs and tables in these establishments are usually well inside the building, or surrounded by a wall.

Being naturally curious people, educated Ethiopians are happy to join foreign friends for a meal at a hotel or restaurant of their choice; these may specialize in Indian, Armenian, Greek, or Italian cuisine, or any number of other cooking styles. Many of the same restaurants will also offer a spicy dish to please their Ethiopian clientele. There are now many fast-food outlets in the Piazza area of Addis Ababa and in Bole.

Less respectable bars, at which mainly alcohol is served and which sometimes double up as brothels, are universally and euphemistically called *buna betoch* ("coffeehouses").

A *talla beit* ("beer house") is where local beer can be purchased in rural areas. Marked by an upturned mug or empty tin placed on top of a pole, they are functional and are not considered disreputable.

SPORTS

Ethiopians are passionate about sports; while they support team games, they excel at individual events such as running.

In middle-class Addis Ababa, tennis and cycling are popular sports. Rally driving has also acquired a loyal following, with an annual rally around the country that begins in Meskel Square, Addis Ababa. In villages, enthusiastic youngsters can be seen swiping a table tennis paddle at the public table. Any child, even in small villages, is likely to be familiar with English Premier League football teams, particular Manchester United and Arsenal. The soccer stadium in Addis Ababa is always full of loyal supporters for matches played there. However, Ethiopia as a nation has not achieved much success recently in this most popular of team games in Africa.

Running as an individual sport is much more successful, and Ethiopia regularly gains a formidable medal haul at the Olympic Games, especially in the 5,000 meter (3.1 miles), 10,000 meter (6.2 miles), and marathon events. Ethiopians are famous throughout the world for their long-distance running and are particularly noted for their "finishing kick," a ferocious finishing sprint. High-profile athletes such as Haile Gebreselassie, Kenenisa Bekele, and Tirunesh Dibaba are not only adored for their achievements, but also for their ability to raise Ethiopia's esteem as a nation. Returning heroes are enthusiastically welcomed home as they step off the airplane, before being paraded down Bole Road. Groups of runners can be seen training on main roads or on the slopes of Entoto, the mountain behind Addis Ababa. The Great Ethiopian Run, a major annual charity event, attracts thousands of participants on a six-mile (ten-kilometer) run around Addis Ababa, which starts and finishes in Meskel Square, in the center of Addis Ababa.

In the countryside there are traditional games that are still played. *Gugs* is played on horseback, where two opposing horsemen rush at each other with lancelike poles and try to unseat the other. This remains popular in the Oromo districts around Addis Ababa.

Genna is a game similar to field hockey, where a ball is hit with sticks by players on opposing sides. This game is especially popular at Christmas, and indeed the name derives from the Amharic name for Christmas.

Being keen horsemen, Ethiopians have also adopted the Western games of polo, show jumping, and racing. In Oromia, weddings will include horsemen riding highly decorated mounts that they will proudly allow to be photographed.

MUSIC AND ART
There is a rich tradition of music, both popular and liturgical, with a number of instruments that reflect regional traditions. These include the *masinko*, a one-stringed instrument played with a bow; the *krar*, or lyre; and the *washint*, or pipe.

These instruments are often played by a musician who also

sings, called an *Azmari*. An *Azmari* will make up songs as he goes, often to suit his audience. In a restaurant or nightclub he will sing songs that are complimentary or insulting to the guests, or skillfully constructed to be both of these at once. This traditional wordplay, known as "wax and gold," is impossible to translate into English.

There is also a large following for bands and singers operating in the cities, using Western instruments such as saxophones. Many of these bands are influenced by traditional rhythms and folk music, but have developed them into a distinctive modern style that has an enthusiastic following among young Ethiopians.

The traditional dance is called *iskestia*, and consists largely of rolling the shoulders to the rhythm of the band.

Liturgical music dates back to a sixth-century Tigrayan, St. Yared. He is considered the father of Ethiopian Church music, inventor of the distinctive chant used in all Orthodox services, and creator of a notation system that predates the Western system. It is a matter of pride to be a member of one of the many church choirs that sing psalms and dance for services.

Modern popular music is now ubiquitous with radio and television, and the bands that feature on them attract a large fan base. As in the West, such innovators and leaders of fashion sometimes have a risqué reputation.

The visual arts are mainly based on the traditional form developed for ecclesiastical use, which is symbolic and two-dimensional in style: every church contains scenes from the Bible, and of the lives of the saints.

There is a growing appreciation among Westernized Ethiopians for the more abstract art practiced by artists who have mainly studied abroad. Some of the better-known galleries in Addis Ababa are the Alliance Française, the Makush Gallery, and the Asni gallery, and many restaurants now hang work by modern Ethiopian artists.

Apart from religious devotional art that sells well, the visual arts (and humanities) are less highly valued than the sciences in the school curriculum.

SHOPPING

Almost anything you need can be bought somewhere in Addis Ababa—except perhaps very specialized goods, such as spare parts for certain vehicles, or artists' materials. Prices of particular goods vary enormously, from those charged in the Mercato market area to high prices at Western-standard supermarkets. Trawling the Mercato demands much stamina and an appreciation of bargaining techniques. It is just as cost-effective to shop at one of the many shopping arcades springing up all over town. Postcards and greetings cards are best bought at a good bookshop, a hotel shop, or the central post office. Ethiopian souvenirs are found in many kiosks behind the central post office and Churchill Avenue.

ATMs are now widespread in Addis Ababa and major cities, and currency can be exchanged in banks and main hotels, but not so easily out of town. Credit cards are not widely used.

PLACES TO GO

In Addis Ababa, do visit the National Museum, which houses the remains of the prehistoric hominid, Lucy; the Museum of the Institute of Ethiopian Studies, located in Addis Ababa University (AAU); the Museum of Natural History, which is in the Science block of AAU; and the Addis Ababa Museum, in an old house on the south side of Meskel Square.

Outside town Ethiopians enjoy various scenic spots where there might also be a café. They may recommend to foreigners, for example, a half-day excursion up Entoto, the mountain behind Addis Ababa; there are two historic churches on top, and views both south across the city and north over the

plains toward the Blue Nile headwaters. They may also suggest a day out to Debre Zeit, an hour's drive south of Addis Ababa, where there are a number of volcanic crater lakes, restaurants, and fruit juice bars.

Lake Langano, about 124 miles (200 km) south of Addis Ababa, is the nearest Ethiopia has to a beach resort. It is now well equipped with hotels, lodges, and camping sites. The water is slightly alkaline and brown in color, but it is safe for swimming.

Ethiopians are less likely to suggest a walk or hike, and taking exercise can be a bother to foreigners because of children who like to pester them. It is not impossible, however. The ridge along Entoto is one possible destination, where walkers are only likely to encounter an athletics team in training, or shy, rather than brazen, children. A walk through the Menagasha forest (located west of Addis Ababa, and requiring a four-wheel drive vehicle), a circuit around the crater lake on the top of Mount Zukwala (near Debre Zeit), or down to the crater lake of Wonchi (near Ambo), are all day outings from Addis Ababa.

Of historical interest for a day out of Addis Ababa is one of the country's most southerly rock-hewn churches, at Adadi Mariam, two hours down the road to Butajira. The Debra Libanos Monastery associated with St. Tekle Haimanot, perched on the side of a gorge in the Blue Nile headwaters, is two hours north on the road to Bahr Dar.

Other main towns also have similar sites of historical and ecclesiastical interest suitable for a weekend away from Addis Ababa. Most have museums. For example, Mekele's main museum is sited in the former palace of Emperor Yohannes IV, and in Jimma, the center of a former sultanate, the museum is devoted to the history of the sultans, and the sultan's "palace," on the edge of town, is open to the public. In Harar, the museum focuses on ethnographic material of the Adari culture. The supposed house of the French poet Rimbaud is preserved, as are the old walls surrounding the

town. Lalibela and Gondar are world famous for their respective rock-hewn churches and castles. Axum is famous for its centuries old stelae, and for being the legendary repository of the original Ark of the Covenant.

There has recently been a huge growth of tourist accommodation to make up for the indifferent service offered during the Derg era. Lodges, both luxurious and simple, have sprung up in some spectacular places, often using traditional designs in an innovative way. These include the Aregash Lodges among the coffee groves at Yirge Alem; the Ankober Palace Lodge, based on Menelik II's old palace, perched on the west scarp of the Rift Valley; and the Gheralta Lodge based near a cluster of rock-hewn churches in Tigray.

BEGGING

The giving of alms is embedded in Ethiopian culture. Well-to-do Ethiopians will always offer money to the obviously infirm, especially outside churches and mosques. Small change should always be carried for this purpose.

Depending on the history of the area and their exposure to foreigners, the local children's reaction to visitors ranges from a shy wave to supplication for sweets (*caramela*), or demands for money. On the whole, this can be resisted with politeness or humor. If necessary, a gift such as fruit or bread can be shared. However, bear in mind that Ethiopians are understandably wise to the *quid pro quo* of having their photograph taken, and foreigners should either respect people's privacy and ask before taking a photograph, or expect to pay something if they do.

Beggars in the street pose a real moral problem to foreigners. Many end up giving to only a few beggars whom they see regularly and have got to know, or they give to charities known to help such people. To give too indiscriminately and too lavishly invites an avalanche of begging. Aware of this problem, the government occasionally clears the streets with some force, but with poverty being what it is, the beggars always return.

TIPPING

In any place, at any time, for any reason, tips
will be expected. Care and discernment,
therefore, are needed if the unwary foreigner
is not to be swamped by expectations.

Tipping in restaurants and cafés is
reasonable. Only the more upscale restaurants
levy a service charge, and customers will tip a
few birr in addition to it—about 5 percent
would be right. Tipping a shared line taxi (see
page 126) or minibus driver is never done,
although it would be expected if you hired a
taxi for the day.

Small change is needed for many small
favors. Generally speaking, if a small boy is
appointed to look after your car the job will
be carried out and he should be paid.
Sometimes the amount might be queried and
only experience will indicate what is fair, and
whether you have the last word.

Often, tourist sites have their own methods
of payment, security, and guides, and it is
worth finding out what they are and keeping
to the prevailing norm when tipping your
guide. Not to do so invites corruption and an
unfair inflation.

chapter seven

TRAVEL, HEALTH, & SAFETY

Ethiopia's transportation system and its health facilities are currently undergoing enormous developments. It is now possible to drive all the way from Addis to Gondar (via Bahr Dar), from Addis to Bale Goba (via Asela or Shashemene), and from Addis to Axum (via Dessie and Mekelle) on asphalted roads, to enter an international standard hospital in Addis Ababa if you are sick, and to stay in a five-star hotel in Addis Ababa. Although the general tourist infrastructure is not as good as in East Africa, the trade-off is that foreigners can experience more closely how Ethiopians live, it is relatively safe, and it is a country that "works."

ETHIOPIANS ON THE MOVE

Ethiopians enjoy exploring their country if they can, and they also like to explore other countries, where they will be self-confident and independent-minded about finding their way. Within Ethiopia there are well-established trade routes that have been used for centuries. Moreover, Christian Ethiopians have long plied the Red Sea, or traveled overland, to make the pilgrimage to Jerusalem. The Queen of Sheba set the most famous precedent when she undertook her visit to King Solomon of Israel to assess his riches. As we have seen in Chapter 3, pilgrimages within Ethiopia are made by both Christians and Muslims to various holy places, involving journeys several days long, often on foot. In addition, diaspora Ethiopians travel to and from their adopted countries, and it is not unusual to hear Canadian and American accents, as well as German or Swedish, spoken by Ethiopians in the departure lounge at the airport.

ARRIVALS

Ethiopian Airlines and other carriers operate flights to Addis Ababa from many places in the world. Visas are required to enter the country, and are available on arrival to citizens of most Western countries. Renewal or extension of a visa can be made at the Immigration Office in the center of Addis Ababa.

Bole Airport, Addis Ababa, is the usual entry point for foreigners, although some may arrive overland from Kenya, at Moyale, or from Sudan, at Metema, but visas are not available at these frontier posts. The frontiers with Eritrea and Somalia are currently closed.

The new Terminal 2 at Bole has many of the modern facilities expected of an international airport. However, most flights in and out are scheduled at roughly the same time in the evening, so it is likely to be crowded at that time and it is important to get into the right lines. Most officials speak good English and they will help you do this. Terminal 1 (the "Old Terminal") handles domestic and some regional flights.

Your first important impression of Ethiopia is likely to be of its bureaucracy in process—usually efficient, but inordinately thorough. First, you need a visa (unless you have obtained one in advance from an Ethiopian embassy), for which you pay a fee of US $20. These are available at the airport only to citizens of certain countries. You then pass through Immigration, where your passport will be stamped with the required period of days or months; check that your visa covers your intended stay, because there is always trouble if you inadvertently overstay your welcome. Lastly, you pass through Customs, which is usually straightforward.

At this point, unless there is someone waiting for you inside the terminal, you will leave the building on your own. Either, hire a porter, who might be waiting just inside the building; or boldly push your cart through the barrier and over the road to the parking garage on the other side, where your contact may be waiting amid the jostling crowd. You can also take a taxi on the other side of the barrier.

If for any reason your flight is delayed, there are well-stocked restaurants and coffee bars in the terminal. It is always useful to have small change in Birr notes, for porters or to pay for airport parking, and coins in case you need to use a public telephone at the airport.

Taxis from the airport are either top of the range yellow taxis, which will take you to the main hotels, or the small, cheaper, blue taxis.

TRANSPORTATION
Ethiopia has all forms of transportation to get about in, and the current frenzy of new road

building equals that carried out by the Italians during their occupation. The train, alas, no longer works, and the national airline, Ethiopian Airlines, with a long and distinguished record, still has the monopoly over all internal air travel.

Planes are quick but they are occasionally unreliable or late, mostly to do with the weather, and local conditions. They will take you to all the main tourist destinations, and a large number of smaller places as well, often leaving at the crack of dawn. Buses are cheaper, and slower, and also leave early from the Mercato Central Bus Station, and are on the whole reliable. There are increasing numbers of luxury coaches called *Selam*, and *Sky*, which leave for such places as Bahr Dar and Mekele from their own stands in different parts of the city. There are also non-luxurious *leoncina* (small buses) that leave the railway station for Debre Zeit and Adama every ten minutes or so.

Within the cities there are blue minibuses known as *minibus,* which operate along fixed routes, advertised by a fare collector, and they do not move from the start of their route until they are full. They offer the best value for getting about town.

There are also blue saloon cars, often Ladas, known as *taxis*, which will take you anywhere for a negotiated fare. However, although there are recognized fares for different journeys, the drivers will more than likely raise the amount for a susceptible foreigner (see opposite).

Green and cream-colored midi-buses, officially known as *Higer Bus*, are new on the streets of Addis Ababa; they take their local name *kendo* from the prominent mirrors at either side of the front that look like the horns of a sheep. The

longer-established, and bigger, red and yellow city buses are often very crowded, though cheap, and people will tell you to be careful of pickpockets in them. In provincial towns there are also motorized rickshaws, called *bajaj*, from the Indian company that manufactures them. These are replacing the horse-drawn *garis*, or carts, formerly used in small towns and villages.

GETTING ABOUT IN TAXIS

There are several grades of taxis, all of which will be waiting at the airport. The most expensive, and most exclusive, is the private taxi that is colored yellow. They will take you anywhere, and they can also be hired at all the main hotels. Fares are standard and should be established in advance. They will be higher at night. A fare across the city can be as much as Birr 250.

The middle grade taxi is a saloon car, often a Lada, painted blue. These can be hired privately, and will usually take you anywhere. They are owned by private individuals or syndicates, and sometimes their roadworthiness shows all the signs of a veteran at the end of a long and honorable career. However, game for anything, they will take all your excess luggage, tied to the roof rack, if necessary. Their drivers will not always speak good English, and their fares need to be well understood and negotiated. It is as well to have a written address, or some idea of where you are going, if you intend to take a taxi to a private house. It is possible to hire these vehicles on a contract basis if you want a cheap, but efficient, means of doing complicated journeys around town.

The most common taxis are people carriers of various sorts, also painted blue. These ply certain routes that the fare collector will shout out at the stops along the way. The routes, and the stops along them, are familiar to habitual travelers, and they are very cheap. There are certain locations that act as a terminus for routes, and these taxis will not usually begin a journey until they are full, so do not expect it to move off straightaway if there is an empty seat next to you. You will normally be asked only for the correct fare for your journey. There is no room for luggage.

GARI AND BAJAJ

Outside Addis Ababa, taxi transport may not be so easy, but *garis*, pulled by rather emaciated looking horses, are very common. Introduced by the Italians during the 1936–41 occupation, these

are now being rapidly replaced by *bajaj*, Indian-made motorized rickshaws. In small towns, when it is hot and there are no modern taxis, *gari* and *bajaj* are the only viable methods of getting about.

RENTING CARS AND BOOKING FLIGHTS

Cars, including four-wheel drive models, can be rented through travel agents or the usual international car rental companies. They are nearly always rented with a driver who will sometimes act as a guide. At the cheaper end of the market the car and driver offered you may well turn out to be a privately owned vehicle, rather than a company one, but they are not necessarily the worse for it. Payments can usually be made in Ethiopian birr, US dollars, or euros.

International or national driver's licenses are not recognized in Ethiopia, or are only valid for one month (local police may not be aware of this). Foreign licenses have to be exchanged for a local one, but it is rarely worth a short-term visitor's time to wait in line for half a day to achieve this. If you have the time or need, you should go to the Addis Ababa Road Transport Authority at Megananya, where your national license will be deposited in return for an Ethiopian license. You should take passport photographs and money to pay for your license. When you leave the country you will need to retrieve your own national license. If you fail to do this, and there is a lapse of time before you renew your local license, your file will be found and you will have to pay retrospective fees.

Flights, both international and domestic, can also be bought at any travel agent. Nonresidents pay a higher rate for domestic flights, which are monopolized by Ethiopian Airlines. These will usually be paid in US dollars. The domestic flights tend not to be as reliable as the international ones for reasons to do with weather, maintenance, or scheduling, so it is as well not to prepare too tight a program based on these flights.

ROADS

Ethiopians generally respect the rules of the road, though the right-hand driving rule might be suspended by drivers faced with a lot of potholes in the road. Wry jokes are made about minibus drivers in Addis Ababa who are always in a hurry, and attention is frequently drawn to the mechanical shortcomings of a car or truck that might pose a danger on the road.

RULES OF THE ROAD
- Drive on the right.
- The speed limit on open roads is 65 mph (110 kmph); in towns it is 25 mph (40 kmph).
- Seat belts are obligatory in all regions.
- Cell phones may not be used while driving.
- Priority is given to vehicles on traffic circles.

Road building is proving to be a real legacy of the present government. Main roads in the country are often now very good, except where they are being rebuilt, which is not uncommon. In this case miles and miles of road works, thick with dust, will be started, but seemingly without any part being finished quickly. The main roads to Bahr Dar, Jimma, Ambo, and Awassa, however, are now all complete. In addition, there has been significant upgrading of other roads, such as that connecting Butajira with Addis Ababa, which is now asphalted.

The same is true in Addis Ababa, where another program of road building, overpass construction, and widening, is also being carried out to improve congestion. However, you may not feel like giving credit for these works when you find that a beautifully smooth divided highway changes in an instant into a rocky obstacle course, giving the impression that someone has walked off for a permanent lunch break leaving a vital piece of road unmade. Particular care, therefore, needs to be taken at night, with signs saying "Careful" looming out of the darkness to catch you unawares, or a pile of rubble left on site, ready to catch your bumpers. The Shanghai Construction Group, which builds overpasses, operates under the slogan, "Science, Cooperation, and Gumption." These are virtues needed to drive in contemporary Addis Ababa and it is not surprising that some foreigners choose in the end to employ a driver to get them about.

However, along with the modernizing of roads, public attitudes are also changing toward

a more responsible use of the roads. Pedestrian
crosswalks are being recognized by pedestrians
for what they are, and drivers are beginning to
slow down on approaching them. In the past, all
pedestrians—who tended to walk on any part of
the asphalt and to drive their animals on it—had
the automatic right of way. Now the law has
established that vehicles driving on the slick, fast,
divided highways have priority (though not on
the other roads) and it is unlawful for stock
owners to haul animals over safety barriers in
order to cross divided highways. Needless to say,
the practice continues, and vigilance is still
needed by drivers to avoid accidents.

Road direction signs are being erected in Addis
Ababa, though they are few and far between. The
blue signs on the ring road are sometimes
aspirational, directing you to where the road will
take you in a few years time. Street signs have also
gone up in the center of town and on the main
roads. Many of these only make sense in relation
to new maps giving the proper names of the
streets. Hitherto, most people knew the roads only
by their nicknames, and, for local people, these
names will be hard to change.

It is still the case that, outside the towns, few
people have access to cars, and their main form of
transport is likely to be a horse or donkey, or their
feet. Crowds of people all walking in one direction
toward a village usually denote market day in
that place. However, ever entrepreneurial local
Ethiopians have mobilized aged Land Rover
vehicles to link remote communities, and

there is a surprisingly good system of buses on other rural roads.

Gasoline (*benzene*) and diesel (*naphta*) are imported, mostly from Sudan, through Metema and Gondar, although some comes from Djibouti. Supplies can run out without apparent reason, and no travel to remote places should be undertaken without taking spare jerricans of fuel and water.

Cars, including four-wheel drive models, can be rented, often with a driver, sometimes on a self-drive basis, from a number of local companies, as well as from Avis, Europcar, and Hertz. There is some lack of clarity as to the validity of foreign driver's licenses in Ethiopia (see page 127), and you are encouraged to trade in your license for an Ethiopian one if you are going to do much driving.

WALKING IN CITIES
Foreigners walking anywhere in Ethiopia tend to attract the attention of crowds of chanting children. They can either be ignored, or turned to advantage, by appointing a guide, setting a fee in advance, and instructing him (usually a male) to keep the others at bay. Apart from this inconvenience, cities are usually safe, and more so with the crowd. However, like any city, there

are areas frequented by pickpockets, areas where foreigners are not particularly welcome, and times of day when it is unwise to be about. It is best to remember that in African cities people tend to watch the world go by and they will remember you, whereas you have hardly noticed them. Most of them will be friendly or benign, but one or two will be looking out for an opportunity.

Ethiopians do not expect foreigners to walk much; indeed it is usually too hot during the day to walk far. If you are seen walking any distance you may well attract the attention of a curious youth wanting to practice his English. However, pure altruism is rare and, inevitably, the youth may well try to push his advantage and obtain something from you, whether information about US green cards, an address, or any other favor.

WHERE TO STAY

There is a very good choice of hotels, ranging from the international standard Sheraton, Hilton, and Intercontinental hotels, all with swimming pools, the more authentically Ethiopian Ghion Hotel with its large gardens and Olympic-sized, heated swimming pool, in the center of Addis Ababa, to humbler hotels mostly in the Bole Road and Churchill Road areas. The bigger hotels all act as hubs for expatriate social life; they also have travel agents and souvenir shops operating inside them. There is adequate public transportation from any of these hotels.

For anyone planning on staying for some time, houses or apartments can be rented through an agent, or by recommendation. Agents can also be found by word of mouth, and there are notice boards at the big hotels and supermarkets serving affluent areas that advertise accommodation, cars, or sales by expatriates leaving the country. Renting a house will certainly involve a contract with payment in advance for several months.

HEALTH
Keeping Clean and Taking Precautions
Ethiopia has no fewer germs than anywhere else, a fact well-known by the locals, who will always bring you a basin of water, soap, and a towel, or show you to a tap to wash your hands before eating. The tap water is cleaner than in most African cities, but it is still advisable to wash all vegetables and fruit in a germicide, and to filter drinking water. Locally bottled water is found everywhere and any café will stock it. During the dry months, when reservoirs are low, tap water may not be available, but warning is usually given and it is as well to keep some jerricans full of water during those times.

Clinics and Hospitals
There are any number of public and private clinics in Addis Ababa and other main towns. Doctors rely on their private practices to make ends meet. Foreigners usually attend private clinics if their embassies have not got a clinic of their own to service their own communities.

Ethiopian doctors often hold private clinics in their area of specialization and, to some extent, you do your own diagnosis, and then find the right doctor. Ethiopian doctors are highly competent, and tend to be among the intellectual elite, but there are not enough of them. There are a number of very good private hospitals in Addis Ababa, such as the Korean Christian Hospital, St. Gabriel's, and the Brass Maternity Hospital. If you break an arm, for example, you should take plenty of money to the hospital, for every part of the diagnosis and treatment will need to be paid for separately. It should be said, however, that Ethiopians tend not to attend clinics and hospitals unless their symptoms are well advanced, and the line in which you are waiting will contain people probably much worse off than you.

Most Ethiopians will also hedge their bets and use traditional healers or medicine. Tapeworm is a very common complaint, and the usual cure for this is a concoction of the toxic flowers of the *kosso*, or *Hagenia abyssinica*, tree.

HIV/AIDS

HIV/AIDS occurs in every town, especially along truck drivers' routes, in brothels, and in garrison towns. The incidence is thought to be an average of 1.5 percent of fifteen to forty-nine year olds, and is higher among women and in urban areas. Ethiopia is relatively proactive in campaigning publicly about it. When somebody dies of AIDS, however, the cause is not usually openly stated, and it would be grossly insensitive to suggest it was so. AIDS tests can be had in most clinics.

LATRINES
Public latrines are so public as to be *en plein air*. There are certain unallocated areas in Addis Ababa where a close eye is needed on the ground when walking, and men do not hesitate to use ditches and fences when the need arises. The situation is so elemental that even citizens from some other African countries will draw attention to this particular shortcoming in Ethiopia.

Indoors, the facilities are sometimes no better, especially in country hotels where the plumbing breaks down and water might be intermittent. Latrines are either seats or, more likely, a "squat" that can be hard on creaky knees. The plumbing is based on the small-bore Italian system that is easily blocked if paper and sundries are flushed down the pipes. Toilet paper should always be taken as none will be found in public places outside Addis Ababa. However, in reputable restaurants or hotels in the main cities, there is no cause for complaint.

SECURITY
Muggings and thefts are not common, but they do happen, and visitors should take sensible precautions. Keep valuables to a minimum (including expensive jewelry and watches), do

not count banknotes openly, keep your hand firmly on your bag, and walk with a companion. Out of town in rural areas some young boys find it good fun to lob stones at foreigners. Lobbing stones toward animals that they are tending is often done to attract their attention or to divert them, and the boys can be very good shots. However, this display of bad manners warrants a vigorous response, or a judicious hasty retreat.

In Addis Ababa pickpockets seem to lurk in the Piazza shopping area and around the General Post Office, and in the Mercato it is wise to take an Ethiopian friend with you to watch out for them. Every house and public building has *zebagnias* (guards), who are sometimes armed. To enter some of the major public buildings, such as the Central Bank or the Hilton Hotel, an X-ray or body search is required. Addis Ababa also teems with a variety of people, some of whom come from countries at odds with Ethiopia's interests, and lethal bombs have been planted in the past in public places and in taxis—Ethiopians themselves are well aware of this particular danger.

There are parts of the country where it is most unwise to go for pleasure: south of Jijiga, in the Ogaden, foreigners run the risk of kidnap or ambush; they are very unlikely to be allowed anywhere near the frontier with Eritrea while the two countries remain hostile.

Elsewhere is generally safe, though not now the Danakil Depression; but, if on a private tour with one's own car, it is essential to ask for local advice in case there are local tensions or particular places where foreigners are unwelcome. The desert area of the Danakil, in any event, should never be entered unless you have adequate water and preferably a local guide. The hottest annual mean temperature on earth was recorded there, at Dallol—94° F (34° C).

In general terms, if you are traveling privately by car, you should check where you are likely to be able to obtain fuel—sometimes it runs out without warning—and take spare jerricans. Spare tires, including a second spare and a repair kit, should also be taken, though *gomistas* (puncture repair shops) are numerous along the main routes. Breakdowns can sometimes be remedied by an innovative mechanic or a passing truck driver but, again, this tends to be on the main routes only.

Valuables
It is not really necessary to have valuables in Ethiopia, unless they are electronic ones. Ethiopians themselves dislike ostentation, and it is bad manners to draw attention to opulence in a

place where most people so obviously cannot obtain the same material goods. However, in Addis Ababa most middle-class and wealthy families will acquire the same gadgets as their counterparts in the West, perhaps more. Valuables should be carefully looked after, or locked away, when not in use, because there are plenty of people who would seize the opportunity to take what they can, even if they have no use for them.

A particular problem has been found at some of the Rift Valley resorts. It has been known for a camera to be taken from the back of a visitor's car while they are unpacking at dusk near Lake Shala with a crowd of onlookers nearby. After a hue and cry is raised the following day, with promises of a reward, the camera then reappears a week later in Addis Ababa, in the care of a young man who may, or may not, be the actual thief. Stories of the reappearance of lost valuables are legion, and serve to show that most people regard stealing as immoral. Most Ethiopians would be deeply embarrassed if this happened to their foreign friends.

Scams
Ethiopians are sometimes adept at trapping visitors in situations where they will feel a moral obligation to pay a lot of money for a service they would rather not have used, or for an article they would rather not have bought. For example, you can be invited to a coffee ceremony, or to see some cultural dancing, then taken on a long

journey to a private house, where after the briefest of cups of coffee, you will be asked a quite outrageous fee. If this happens to you, pay 100 Birr at most, and take your leave.

Do not go on long journeys by car with strangers to unknown parts of the city. Try to avoid engaging with unofficial guides around the main tourist hotels. Remember that changing money unofficially can get you into trouble, resulting, at least, in the confiscation of your money; for an Ethiopian it would be imprisonment.

chapter eight

BUSINESS BRIEFING

THE BUSINESS ENVIRONMENT

Ethiopia is home to a number of old established businesses, and a growing number of successful new companies. During the latter years of Emperor Haile Selassie's reign, which ended in 1974, there was real expansion in the Ethiopian economy. Many companies started during those years survived the Marxist regime that followed, though many others were nationalized and run down. Since the advent in 1991 of the present government, there has been a broadly free market economy, albeit within the framework of a "developmental state" policy—a form of state-guided capitalism. The economy has grown particularly vigorously in the last decade, and there has been huge expansion in the banking, construction, and agriculture sectors.

The present Ethiopian government is committed to a policy of "agriculture-led industrialization." In recent years there has been a determined attempt to attract foreign investors to the country, and to attract Ethiopians in the diaspora to return home with their capital and their business skills. Women entrepreneurs are now making considerable inroads into what was once a male-dominated sector.

Ethiopia's principal exports are coffee, leather, sesame seed, and other grains and pulses, and, more recently, cut flowers. *Chat* is also a major informal export commodity. Foreign exchange is earned through the provision of services to Addis Ababa's vast diplomatic community, based around the headquarters of the United Nations Economic Commission for Africa, and the African Union. Ethiopian Airlines is a rapidly expanding, and highly profitable company. There is a small but growing tourist industry, and there will soon be exports of hydroelectric power. Nonetheless, the value of imports greatly exceeds that of exports, and from time to time there are acute shortages of foreign exchange.

There are several types of enterprise in modern Ethiopia. Parastatal monopolies, dating back to Imperial and Marxist days, and now referred to as state-owned enterprises, are often more efficient than you might expect. Ethiopian Airlines and the Ethiopian Electric Power Corporation are among the front-runners. By contrast, Ethiopian Telecommunications (ETC), the shipping companies, various state-owned banks, and the Addis Ababa Water Authority attract more criticism, but provide an adequate if not a sparkling service. ETC's stranglehold on Internet services, which are very poor and expensive, provokes widespread resentment. Despite this, the state seems determined to hang on to control of the country's basic economic and security infrastructure.

There is also a number of "parapartatal" companies—that is, companies owned by endowment funds linked to political parties in the ruling coalition. These companies have investments in textiles, engineering, import and export of coffee and grains, drip irrigation, pharmaceuticals, and much else besides. There are occasional complaints that these companies enjoy favored status in access to bank loans, and to government contracts. These complaints are routinely rebutted by government sources.

In other areas, liberalization has spawned a number of new privately owned banks, insurance companies, flower and coffee exporters, and service providers, to join the surviving privately owned companies that managed to escape nationalization before 1991.

The Midroc Group of companies and associated businesses, all partly or wholly owned by Sheikh Mohammed Al-Amoudi, an Ethiopian born investor with connections to Yemen, Saudi Arabia, and Sweden, form something of a special case, as they dwarf every other foreign investment by a factor of several times. These investments include gold mining, hotels, construction materials, food production, and much else. They also include Dashen Bank, Ethiopia's second-largest commercial bank.

Other banks often have loose and unacknowledged connections to regional states or to particular Ethiopian nationalities: Nib International Bank is Gurage-focused; Wagagen Bank is more Tigray-oriented; and there are three banks linked with the development of Oromia.

Businesses and government offices tend to be open Monday through Friday from 8:30 a.m. to

5:30 p.m., with a lunch break of up to an hour. This break starts at 11:30 a.m. on Fridays to allow Muslim employees to attend midday prayers at the mosque. Retail

businesses, and most banks, are also open on Saturday mornings.

INVESTING IN ETHIOPIA

Foreign investment in the Ethiopian economy is encouraged, and it is relatively easy to set up an enterprise, either as wholly foreign-owned company or as a joint venture. If you seek to do business in Ethiopia, and accept the constraints of the culture, you can make good profits. The Ethiopians will hope that you retain those profits, at least in part, inside the country. If you are ready to become a member of the Ethiopian business community you will be welcomed.

Foreign investors will find it worth visiting the Ethiopian Investment Commission on Bole Road, Addis Ababa. This organization provides a shortcut through the bureaucracy to anyone seeking to set up a business. It provides work permits, residence permits, trade licenses, and company registrations. It also advises on what you may and may not do, what sectors of the economy are open to investment, and so on.

INVESTMENT: A QUICK GUIDE

Although regulations change from time to time, here are some broad guiding principles:

- No foreigners may invest in banking, insurance, telecommunications, or large-scale aviation.
- Foreigners who are Ethiopian by birth may invest in a wider range of activities than other foreigners.
- Foreigners who do not seek the tax privileges and guarantees associated with an official foreign investment may operate as domestic investors along with anybody else.
- A minimum of US $200,000 is required for a wholly foreign owned investment, and US $150,000 for a joint venture with an Ethiopian. There is no minimum percentage for the equity participation of the Ethiopian partner in a joint venture.

Once you have taken the plunge, what follows may well be both challenging and profitable.

THE BUSINESS CULTURE

Ethiopian businesspeople are said to have an aversion to risk. This is understandable; they have plenty of risks to be averse to. Over the years some of the country's most prominent entrepreneurs and business executives have spent months or even years behind bars, accused of corruption offenses for which they have never formally been charged, or for which they have been finally and belatedly exonerated. Influence and power within organizations such as the Chambers of Commerce and the Confederation of Ethiopian Labor Unions (CELU) are often subject to political forces that foreigners do not understand.

The tendency to mistrust and question people's motives, which underlies so much of Ethiopian culture, is prominent in business culture, too. There is a fear that contracts will be unenforced, that promises will not be kept. As a consequence many transactions are in cash; personal or company checks are not commonly accepted, and when used will generally be cashed within an hour or two of receipt. Credit card transactions are very rare. People tend to prefer to do business with old and trusted associates, or at the very least to spend time building a relationship with a new acquaintance, before they will go very far in negotiating a contract.

In practice, a business relationship may begin with an introduction, followed by a meeting in a coffee shop—on neutral territory. This  may last up to an hour. Then, if it is established that business of mutual benefit is at least possible, an invitation to an office or production facility will be suggested. Lunch may be taken at a local restaurant, and slowly and very politely a visiting businessperson will be assessed. Ethiopians are often extremely shrewd judges of character; if they think you are straightforward and have integrity, you can look forward to a long and rewarding association. If not, you will be politely dropped.

You may have the misfortune to meet altogether dodgier characters if you have no introduction to mainstream business networks. These types scout for investment partners from overseas, hoping to secure very large cash investments in return for a very small shareholding. They often claim access to, or influence with, regional authorities, or to vast tracts of agricultural land. Be wary of anyone seeking to push you into a quick contract; and refrain from making even a verbal agreement that you will be held to. Honest agreements in Ethiopia are nearly always carefully thought through, and are almost invariably in writing.

Direct corruption or bribery in Ethiopia is not that common. If it occurs in a business transaction, and is discovered, the legal penalties can be severe. More subtle forms of corruption, such as under-invoicing or over-invoicing, can also lead a foreigner into deep waters. Much more common is the asking of a favor once a deal has been done. This may be anything from the purchase of a laptop computer, to the provision of fees to a second cousin for higher education in Canada or Australia. Similarly, a request for assistance in obtaining a visa for a relative to a European country or to North America, by providing a letter of invitation, for example, is not uncommon.

LEGALITIES
The civil and commercial codes of Ethiopia are available in print in English, and are a useful resource. These are broadly based on the Napoleonic Code.

Companies, which may be either Share Companies, or Private Limited Companies, are easy enough to form and register. They are regulated by the federal and regional ministries of Trade and Industry, in accordance with the provisions of the Ethiopian Commercial Code. No business may operate without a trade license, which has to be renewed annually.

It is important to get employment contracts carefully written and signed; otherwise difficulties will arise with your workforce at a later date. This can lead to court actions.

The legal process is very slow in Ethiopia, which tends to make contracts unenforceable in practice, if not in theory. This can lead to late payment and other difficulties. It is as well therefore to include in any contract some agreement to arbitration, short of recourse to the courts. It is wise to develop a relationship of trust with Ethiopian colleagues, but at the same time to write contracts clearly and carefully.

EXCHANGE CONTROL

The Ethiopian currency is called the Birr, divided into 100 centimes, known in Amharic as *santim*.

In 2013 the value of the Birr was approximately 18 to the US dollar. The Birr has depreciated against the dollar very slowly over the years. Its value against all other currencies depends on the current value of the US dollar. Although investors are allowed to maintain accounts in hard currencies, exchange control regulations are quite complex and are strictly enforced. At times of foreign exchange shortage, it may take weeks or months to open a letter of credit, or to repatriate dividends.

There is also a parallel market for foreign exchange, in cash, operating illegally. Many people use this market, but it is not for the inexperienced, and if caught, prosecution can follow.

BUREAUCRACY

Ethiopian bureaucracy is extremely efficient, if sometimes slow. You will encounter it if you need a driver's license, insurance coverage, a bank account, or a residence permit.

File keeping is meticulous and officials of all ranks are generally helpful. Any operation, from cashing a check in a bank, to renewing a driver's license, will involve half a dozen people handling your request, issuing invoices and receipts, and processing and receiving money. All will do their work methodically, and you will generally come away with your business completed relatively quickly, unless you have the misfortune to hit a tea or lunch break, a staff meeting, or a training day. In this case nothing will happen until everyone gets back to their desks.

MEETINGS
Dress

You may be surprised to see that only the most senior people in a ministry or a commercial company will be very smartly dressed. However, if you are going to meet someone at the top of an enterprise, you should be prepared to be smartly dressed yourself. For men, this means a suit and a tie, and neatly polished shoes; for women a greater variety of dress is possible. It used to be unacceptable for women to wear trousers. It is fair to say that this is no longer the case.

Etiquette

Ethiopians are a polite people, and will always rise to greet a visitor to their office. They will shake hands, and invite you to take a seat, before they attend to your business. They will generally address you by your title (Mr., Mrs., Dr., Reverend, or whatever), in conjunction with your first name, rather than your surname, and will expect the same from you. Government ministers and senior businessmen will certainly expect to be called *Ato* (Mr.), *Woizero* (Mrs.), or *Woizerit* (Miss), and if they have a doctorate to be addressed as *Doctor*. For ambassadors and ministers the use of "Your Excellency" is appropriate. Orthodox and Catholic Bishops are "Your Beatitude," and the Orthodox Patriarch is "Your Holiness."

It is conventional in Ethiopia to open the conversation with an exchange of polite questions along the lines of "How are you, are you well?" followed by inquiries about your family. Once this dialogue is concluded, you can get down to discussion of the main subject of your meeting. It is important not to skip the preliminaries.

Making Your Case

Ethiopian businesspeople will respond well to an articulate, clearly reasoned, verbal presentation of

your proposal. Technical presentations from a
laptop computer may also be of help. People will
listen attentively until you have finished, and then
respond. You may then converse, and exchange
views until both parties feel they are of one mind. If
you are the person to whom a proposal is being
presented, bear in mind that you are not expected
to interrupt during the initial presentation, but to
save your questions until later.

Negotiations

If a discussion concerns a price, you may have to
compromise and bargain, so you might as well start
by asking for somewhat more than you expect to
receive. The tone should be polite and never
confrontational.

Don't expect decisions to be made on the spot.
These are often made behind the scenes and you may
be asked back several times before receiving a reply.

Disagreements should never involve raised voices.
You may find at the end of a meeting that your point
has been taken silently, if not overtly. Try to find ways
to compromise, even at the cost of delay. Remember
that Ethiopians are extremely patient, and that they
always believe that time is on their side. You may be
the one who is leaving on an airplane early the next
morning, and you will be at a disadvantage. Don't be
afraid to use delaying tactics yourself.

CONTRACTS AND FULFILLMENT

Should disagreement arise over fulfillment of a
contract it is as well to remember that litigation is

an Ethiopian national sport. It is very hard to do anything in Ethiopia without an occasional brush with the courts, since anybody who is aggrieved will bring a civil action as a first rather than a last resort.

It is normally wise to seek a settlement out of court, which is easy enough to do, through the traditional system of adjudication by "elders." Each party appoints two or three "elders," or representatives, who need not be old, but should at least hold a position in society, who will meet and recommend a settlement. If that is acceptable, the court case is withdrawn.

If an out of court settlement cannot be reached, legal process and appeals to higher courts can take several years to conclude.

WOMEN ENTREPRENEURS

The rise of many women to the top in business, law, and politics is a feature of modern Ethiopia. They will expect to be treated by men as equals, and if they are in senior positions they are likely to be both tough and decisive. They have been helped on their way, despite the constrictions of traditional culture, by the passion of Ethiopians for modernity. They have also been helped by the presence in Addis Ababa of a vast array of international organizations, which have brought contemporary standards of equal employment to the country. Women with power and influence are now a permanent feature of the Ethiopian scene.

chapter **nine**

COMMUNICATING

LANGUAGE

The official language of the federal Ethiopian government is Amharic, or *Amarinya,* a member of the South Semitic language family. It is widely

used as a *lingua franca*, is the official language of Addis Ababa, and of several Southern and Western regional states, and was once universally taught in schools as the national language. Amharic is a grammatically complex and subtle language, and is hard for outsiders to learn really well, but the effort to learn just a few words will be useful and widely appreciated.

Amharic is written in Ge'ez script, derived from an ancient South Arabian alphabet. It is written from left to right and each letter represents a syllable, consisting of a basic consonant with a vowel added to it. There are more than 224 possible written letters, made up by multiplying each of thirty-two consonants by seven variants, denoting the following vowel sound. The total number varies slightly depending on which of Ethiopia's Semitic languages the alphabet is used for. One of Ethiopia's grand traditions is the priest's school in which small children learn these letters—so if you pass through a churchyard, and hear children chanting "*Ha Hu Hi Ha He Huh Ho*", they are hard at work on the alphabet, or *fidel*.

Learning Amharic

If you are staying long-term in Ethiopia, and would like to make a serious attempt to master the language, including the alphabet, it is probably best to combine formal classes in grammar with informal conversation, and a great deal of rote learning. There are numerous  agencies providing classes in Amharic, and any number of private tutors. Courses are widely available, especially through the seminary of the Mekane Yesus Church, and the Italian Cultural Institute. There are also a number of phrase books available in bookshops, and there are courses available for sale on CDs.

A FEW HANDY WORDS

If you are less ambitious linguistically, but would still like to have a few words, buy a phrase book and ask for help from those you meet. Here are some words to get you started:

Awon, or *Ow* – yes

Ai – no

Alla – there is

Yelem – there isn't

Ishi – OK

Ebakeh (male), *Ebakesh* (female), *Ebakwo* (polite) – please

Amesegenalehu or *Egziabheristilign* – thank you

Tenayistilign – hello

Indimin neh (male), *Indimin nesh* (female),
   Indimin not (polite) – how are you?

Dehna, Egziabher Yimesgen – well, thanks be to God

At first sight the basic greetings, and the words for "thank you" and "please," appear something of a mouthful, but you will soon get the hang of them. Be aware that different forms are used when addressing males or females, or persons to whom you wish to show respect.

Other Languages

Ge'ez is an ancient language, no longer spoken but still used as the liturgical language of the Orthodox Church. Its closest modern descendant is Tigrinya, spoken in Tigray and Eritrea. Amharic and Gurage also derive from Ge'ez.

Other regional languages in official regional use include Afan Oromo, used in Oromia; Somali, in Somali Region; Afar in Afar Region; and Adare, spoken in Harar. Many of these languages are now written in a Latin script, which occasionally gives unexpected values to familiar letters. Thus, a hotel in Somali is *Xooteel*, where "x" represents the "h" sound; and *Maxamed* represents the common name Mohammed. In Afan Oromo, however, "x" represents a voiced "t" sound, and "q" a voiced "k" sound, both consonants having a sort of "click" sound.

Foreign Languages

English is the most widely used foreign language. Many Ethiopians speak it fluently, particularly educated people from before the time of the Derg, and, of course, those who have been brought up abroad. An Ethiopian educated within the country will speak thoughtfully, deliberately, and often softly, and the accent will be similar to English spoken in the Middle East.

Because English has been the medium of education for so long, certain particularly Ethiopian English idioms have acquired currency in the country. "Are you fine?" will be commonly used in place of "Are you well?" If you knock on a door, you may well hear the response "Get in," rather than "Come in."

Ethiopians, with their connections to the diaspora in North America and Europe, are now likely to speak a range of languages other than their own or English. Older people who had connections with the former Italian colony of Eritrea, or who remember the occupation of 1936–41, may understand basic Italian. Many Italian words have also entered the Amharic language, for example *macchina* (car), or *mercato* (market). There is also an Italian community school from which Ethiopians have graduated.

In the southeast, close to the former French colony of Djibouti and alongside the French-built Djibouti–Addis Ababa railway, many people know French, and you can safely say *au revoir* in Harar and people will understand.

The French Lycée Guebre Mariam in Addis Ababa has educated very many Ethiopians alongside Francophone expatriates, adding French to the several languages Ethiopians might speak. Its influence is reinforced by the thriving French cultural center, the Alliance Française, which has a strong interest in historical and archaeological studies. French words that have entered Amharic include *la gare* (railway station).

There are also words of Greek origin in Amharic, such as *terapeza* (table) and *pappas* (bishop), which were introduced long ago.

The foreign language that has had the longest association with Ethiopia is Arabic. Many traders use this language, especially those of Yemeni or Saudi origin. Very many words are common, or similar, to both Arabic and Amharic—for example, *faras* (horse), *muz* (bananas), and *birtukan* (oranges, or "Portugal fruit").

FORMS OF ADDRESS AND BODY LANGUAGE

When addressing someone, on the telephone or in the flesh, whether in English or Amharic, it is polite to use *Ato* (Mr.), *Woizero* (Mrs.), *Woizerit* (Miss), followed by that person's first name. Thus Ethiopia's current prime minister, Hailemariam Desalegn, would be addressed as *Ato Hailemariam* and not *Mr. Desalegn*. Desalegn is his father's given name.

Ethiopians go through life with their personal or given name, followed by their father's first name. Sometimes, they may also add their paternal grandfather's name if there is likely to be confusion. Married women never take their husband's name.

When greeting a person in the flesh, it is normal to bow slightly while you shake hands. This is done by placing the left hand on the right wrist as you shake. A person who feels greatly subservient will offer a wrist, not a hand. If you are seated you should make at least a halfhearted attempt to rise to your feet to greet a newcomer. The person entering the room will almost certainly protest politely before you reach the standing position.

In Amharic it is conventional to ask several times how you are, and to reply that you are well. This occasionally comes into English as "How are you? Are you fine? Fine, thanks be to God." Close friends of the same sex, or the opposite sex, may kiss each other three or four times on both cheeks on meeting after a period apart.

Ethiopians can be tactile. If you see two traffic policemen holding hands, it does not mean they are gay, merely close friends. The sight of men and women holding hands is increasingly common in the city, but is still considered a bit "forward."

It is normal in Ethiopia to stand somewhat closer to another person when waiting in line for a bus than you would in the West. Nevertheless, bumping into another person in the street is not polite, and you should always say *yikirta* (excuse me) if this happens.

GOOD MANNERS, RETICENCE, AND SOCIAL NUANCES

After the initial greetings and mutual expressions of interest in the health of the other, it is usual to be somewhat circumspect in one's inquiries. It would be considered impolite to go straight into one's own agenda, not to say unwise, for it is more productive to explore obliquely the agenda of the other before putting your case.

Ethiopians rarely raise their voice in anger with others. Foreigners who do this invite either a sullen response, because Ethiopians hate to be shamed in front of other people, or the derision reserved for those who lack self-control.

On meeting a group of people it is polite to acknowledge all of them, including the driver or maid, with a handshake. On entering a house, any servants present should be acknowledged when you meet your host.

In general conversation Ethiopians tend to be reticent about their personal circumstances, a habit borne of generations of experience of living under authoritarian regimes, and in a competitive atmosphere where jobs are hard to come by. Family information, personal tragedies, and the like, is unlikely to be volunteered. Some imagination is needed, therefore, on the basis of age, region, and politics, to guess someone's personal history and to be sensitive. Many families have lost a member through war, or during the Derg regime, or have relatives in exile or who are economic migrants.

When inviting Ethiopians from diverse walks of life to one party, great care should be taken in bringing them together. The factors that might divide one Ethiopian from another are not just based on region; there are also class and ideological differences that are as subtle as the British class system. Do not assume, for example, that a prominent Tigrayan will enjoy the company of a prominent Oromo at your dinner table. Political passions and loyalties run very deep.

Nor should you expect a well qualified young person to be a good leader in a society where great respect is given to older people.

HUMOR
Ethiopians have a good sense of humor beneath their rather sober and self-controlled exterior. They thoroughly enjoy banter using wit and pun. At a more basic level they love slapstick and, while they might sympathize, they would still laugh at a friend's misfortune, say, if he fell off a horse. They would not be so rude as to laugh at a stranger's misfortune, and they would be deeply sympathetic if the misfortune were illness or financial.

Ethiopian humor comes out in using odd names for common things. We have seen that the new Chinese midi-buses with very prominent mirrors hanging over the windshield are called *kendo,* "horns" in Amharic, because they look like sheep's horns. The special yellow taxis that go only to the airport are called "President," because Ethiopia's mainly ceremonial head of state is thought to spend his days going to and from the airport to meet foreign dignitaries.

THE MEDIA

The government radio broadcasts in several local languages, as well as in English, and there are now private stations broadcasting in Amharic. There are many current affairs programs, phone-in programs, and news bulletins, and songs and music in addition.

The television comes in two channels, both run by government-owned Ethiopian Television. Those who have access to satellite television, which includes many bars and hotels, will also watch CNN, BBC World, and numerous sports channels. It is quite normal to leave the television on during a meal at home, and for it to be on in the background in hotels and restaurants.

Newspapers are generally in English, Amharic, or Afan Oromo. The best-known English tabloid weeklies are *Capital*, *Fortune*, and *The Reporter*. The government publishes the *Ethiopian Herald* as a broadsheet, and there are increasing numbers of magazines available, some lasting only for one or two issues. Boys in the street will often sell *Time, Newsweek*, or *The Economist* to people sitting in their cars at traffic lights. These may be recycled copies. There are surprisingly few other foreign newspapers.

The press mainly operates on the principle of intelligent self-censorship. If any newspaper goes too far in criticism of government policy, or of powerful personalities, it may be closed down, and the editor arrested. This does not mean that the papers are not free to disagree politely with official policy, but it does mean that there is little deep investigative journalism, and that if criticism is made it is often by oblique means. A speech from an opposition figure or an Eritrean government spokesman may be printed in full, alongside a forthright condemnation by the editor of the opinions expressed. This way it will have been printed, without risk of condemnation.

THE TELEPHONE

Telephones (*silk*, in Amharic) are now widespread, and all are operated by Ethio Telecom, known as Tele. As well as domestic and business landlines, Tele provides blue public telephones, sometimes in telephone boxes, all over the country; you need to buy a phone card to work them. Landlines begin with 01, 02 up to 08, followed by a further eight digits. You have to dial all ten digits to make a call.

Cell phones, on the other hand, begin with 09. These are becoming increasingly easy to obtain, and are often a more reliable means of contacting someone. They now work in towns and villages in much of the countryside, though there are still frequent network problems. Cell phones are charged using plastic charge cards purchased for 25, 50, or 100 Birr. To use them you key in the formula *805*, then the hidden number from the charge card, then #, and finally press the dial key. The phone tells you what to do, but in Amharic. Some, though not all, European cell phones will work in Ethiopia using the roaming facility. Vodafone works, as does O2, but Orange does not. Using your home cell phone in Ethiopia is very expensive.

Neither landlines nor cell phones offer a messaging service, unless they are landlines attached to an answering machine. The best way to leave a message on a cell phone is to send a text message. It may be useful to have an Amharic speaker on hand to help with translation should you get through to a non-English speaker.

Tele has offices in all medium-sized towns, where you can make a call. It publishes a phone book, but it is hard to obtain. The standard international dialing codes, prefixed by 00, will enable you to dial the world. Tele also has the ability to switch off services, such as SMS, if a national security issue arises.

THE INTERNET

Tele monopolizes the Internet service in Ethiopia. Internet use is largely confined to the cities and larger towns, but is not widespread. It is technically illegal to Skype out of the country, and Internet cafés won't have the facility, but it is difficult to prevent private users Skyping in.

The Internet service is heavily overworked, and dial-up is slow. Broadband can be found in the big hotels but is very expensive. Wireless connections are available in international hotels, and in one or two favored locations—for example, at the Swiss Café, between Bole Medhane Alem Church and the Ring Road, and the Lime Tree Café in Bole Road. Ethiopia's Internet domain is .et.

The Internet, for those fluent in English, has opened up Ethiopia to the world. As well as being used for information gathering, the Web is used for expressing opinions. There are numerous political Web sites both hostile to the government and supportive of it, and a number of them use extremely abusive language. Opposition sites are often censored, but can be accessed from the USA or Europe by backdoor means.

The slowness and expense of the Internet is often seen as a national scandal, and there are frequent calls for the privatization of Tele, or for alternative service providers. So far, these have met deaf ears in the government.

THE POST OFFICE

The post office, or Posta Bet, is a venerable institution that delivers letters efficiently and cheaply to P.O. boxes in post offices throughout the country, but not to domestic addresses.

Post boxes are found outside post offices, and are painted yellow. To rent a P.O. box, you pay a small annual fee, in return for which you are given your own key to a specific, numbered, box; you are expected to collect your letters yourself. If you receive a parcel, a note will be left in the box; to collect it, you will need to bring a passport to identify yourself (therefore beware of the European custom of using a woman's husband's name on envelopes) and pay any necessary customs dues.

However, as everywhere, the post office is losing customers to the Internet. Courier companies like DHL and UPS also deliver and receive documents and parcels, which often have to be collected from their offices.

CONCLUSION

Ethiopia's diversity makes generalization extremely difficult. It is a nation comprising several nations; it is at once African and Middle Eastern; it is both traditional and modern; it has fast-moving cities with the latest gadgets, and rural areas set in a time warp. Underlying its various cultures, however, is a deep awareness of their shared history, which is a source of pride and which contributes to a sense of unity and nationhood.

If national character can be generalized then the Ethiopians are proud, with a strong desire to be modern. They are self-controlled, courteous, and polite toward outsiders, yet have a strong sense of their own moral superiority, and can be somewhat secretive. They are a nation of individualists, making them superb athletes but not team players. Lovers of systematic government, they will find every means to add to their already heavy bureaucracy.

But if you show respect for their culture and earn their trust, you will find that in an Ethiopian there is always an intelligent partner who is willing to look at problems in a new way, who is both a hardworking colleague and a loyal friend.

Further Reading

Archaeology
Phillipson, David W. *Ancient Ethiopia. Aksum: Its Antecedents and Successors.* London: British Museum Press, 1995.

Church
Grierson, Roderick (ed.). *African Zion, The Sacred Art of Ethiopia.* USA: Yale University Press, 1993.

Fiction
Gibb, Camilla. *Sweetness in the Belly.* Canada: Heinemann, 2006.

Laird, Elizabeth and Yosef Kebede. *When the World Began: Stories Collected in Ethiopia.* Oxford: Oxford University Press, 2000.

Ayele, Negussay. *Wit and Wisdom of Ethiopia.* Los Angeles: Tsehai Publishers, 2003.

Geography and Travel
Morell, Virginia. *Blue Nile: Ethiopia's River of Magic and Mystery.* USA: National Geographic Society, 2002.

Smedley, Philip. *The Chains of Heaven: An Ethiopian Romance.* London: HarperCollins, 2005.

Murphy, Dervla. *In Ethiopia with a Mule.* London: John Murray, 1968.

Thesiger, Wilfred. *The Danakil Diary: Journeys through Abyssinia, 1930–34.* UK: Flamingo, 1998.

History
Henze, Paul B. *Layers of Time: A History of Ethiopia.* USA: Palgrave Macmillan, 2004.

Zewde, Bahru. *A History of Modern Ethiopia 1855-1991.* Oxford: James Currey, 2002.

Pankhurst, Richard. *The Ethiopians: a History.* Oxford: Blackwell, 1998.

Rankin, Nicholas. *Telegram from Guernica: The Extraordinary Life of George Steer, War Correspondent.* London: Faber, 2003.

Natural History
Perlo, Ber van. *Birds of Eastern Africa: Collins Illustrated Checklist.* London: Collins, 1995.

Demissew, Sebsebe and Inger Nordal, Odd E Stabbetorp. *Flowers of Ethiopia and Eritrea: Aloes and Other Lilies.* Addis Ababa: Shama Books, 2003.

Travel Guides
Phillips, Matt and Jean-Bernard Carillet. *Ethiopia and Eritrea Travel Guide.* Melbourne/Oakland/London/Paris: Lonely Planet Publications, 2006.

Briggs, Philip. *Ethiopia.* Chalfont St. Peter, Bucks.,England: Bradt, 2009.

Useful Web Sites

www.thisisaddis.com
Cultural information with bias on music

www.addisallaround.com
General cultural information

www.waltainfo.com
Government-sponsored news site

www.ethiopianreporter.com
Independent news site

culture smart! ethiopia

Index

Acknowledgments

Best thanks to my sons, Patrick and Francis, for their research, to my husband Charles, whose insights as a foreigner in Ethiopia were invaluable, and to my innumerable Ethiopian friends, both inside and outside the country, for their patient tuition in things Ethiopian. Without them I would know nothing. This work is entirely my responsibility.